LEARNING FOR

Ownership

Dr. Linda J. Black,
Congratulations on
your Associate professor-
ship, on your passion
for quality education,
and on your support of
Learning for Ownership.

Margaret Ford Fisher

MARGARET FORD FISHER

LEARNING FOR

Ownership

Empowering African American

Students for Success in a

Twenty-First Century Society

TATE PUBLISHING
AND ENTERPRISES, LLC

Published by Tate Publishing & Enterprises, LLC
127 E. Trade Center Terrace | Mustang, Oklahoma 73064 USA
1.888.361.9473 | www.tatepublishing.com

Tate Publishing is committed to excellence in the publishing industry. The company reflects the philosophy established by the founders, based on Psalm 68:11,
"The Lord gave the word and great was the company of those who published it."

Book design copyright © 2011 by Tate Publishing, LLC. All rights reserved.
Cover design by Kenna Davis
Interior design by Joel Uber

Published in the United States of America

ISBN: 978-1-61346-741-1
Education: Multicultural Education
11.10.03

Dedication

This book is dedicated to the memory of my parents, Mr. and Mrs. Henry and Margaret Bell Billingsley Fincher.

Acknowledgments

I acknowledge my husband, Judge Raymond Lamar Fisher, who has provided extraordinary encouragement and support to me throughout the development of this work. His knowledge and wisdom have been constant sources of strength. Conversations with him throughout the preparation of this work have added greater clarity to my perspectives. I love him for the person that he is and the role that he plays in the lives of children. Additionally, I acknowledge my siblings, who are also bearers of the torch for education, and to my youngest brother – Eddie Dean – who, in his own right, has scaled great heights in education and continues to make a significant difference in the lives of young people.

I extend sincere thanks to the students that I have been privileged to teach over the years whose quests for a quality education have been nothing short of remarkable. I commend and thank the National Alliance of Black School Educators and the National Caucus of Black School Board Members for their advocacy on behalf of African American children to improve educational quality and equity. I also thank them for recognizing my work and awarding me the W. E. B. DuBois Education Award.

Finally, to the staff of TATE Publishing, I am eternally grateful for the demonstrated excellence displayed throughout the production process to develop a resource for practitioners that can help transform lives for generations to come.

Table of Contents

Part Two

123

Part Three

215

Setting the Stage

Be ye therefore transformed by the renewing of your mind.
Romans 12:2

African American children are not being prepared academically to compete in a twenty-first century global society. This is an age of digital literacy, inventive thinking, mathematical competency, and technical acumen. This is an age where "knowledge is power." Yet, most African American children are not acquiring the knowledge or the skills required for success. The dropout rates are too high. The educational preparedness is too low. The ability for work or college after high school graduation is too uncertain due to students' poor workforce and college-readiness skills. What can be done to shift the momentum and to turn the tide? Solutions that can be implemented immediately will be addressed in this book.

Like a crescendo, this book will build in its momentum to the grand conclusion. But first, it is essential to start at the beginning and tap, piece by piece, into what is needed to help African American children succeed and what is needed to reinvigorate society. So, let us begin.

This book is about surmounting the challenges in urban education to create more robust student learning outcomes among African American children. It explores what motivates children to learn and the basic instinct that resides within each child to do more, to be more, and to achieve more. It also provides a typology of student disposition, a student survey profile, and an empowerment model that can be utilized to prepare more African American youth for success in a highly technological and global age. While many studies show how some students have progressed through the educational system and achieved success and a prosperous life, other studies show how many African American youth are languishing, either unemployed, working in semi-skilled jobs, or serving time in prison. With high attrition rates, low performance rates, and low graduation rates, the gnawing question is, Why? Why do some students, exposed to challenging conditions, succeed and why do others fail? Families have asked the same question about their children. How is it that siblings raised by parents under similar conditions differ so greatly in their values, aspirations, and abilities? Why do some children drop out of school and others persist? Obviously, the reasons vary. Without citing the academic reasons why, at this time, it is clear that great achievements and a fulfilled life begin first in the mind of each individual child.

What do African American children think about? What do they think about themselves, about their abilities, and about their opportunities? What is their level of exposure to the magnificence that abounds in life? Is the exposure for the masses limited to blight and despair? If so, what do they think about and what do they hope for? Are the achievers the only ones who escape the enslavement and captivity of the slums, the urban blight, and the despair? How does the general view that African American male children have of themselves and of their place in society differ from that of other male children or even from that of African American female children? The questions are compelling, but the beginning point to the answer remains the same: renew the minds of the children.

The premise of this book is grounded in two primary beliefs: 1) transforming the mindsets and the skill sets of African American children will create a new attitude and a new set of beliefs that will greatly improve their performance in school, their overall persistency and completion rates, and their chances for success in life, and 2) providing practitioners with the proper empowerment tools to teach African American children will result in the attainment of higher performance and accountability ratings for schools.

The process of transforming the mindset pertains to what the child thinks, what the child believes, what the child is taught, and what the child reads, hears, sees, feels, and experiences both in and out of school. The process of transforming the skill set pertains to preparing the child (Pre-K through 12ᵗʰ grade) for a wholesome life by teaching the core competencies that are essential to his success academically, personally, and interpersonally. In order for the educational system to positively impact African American children's lives in a significant way, practitioners must understand the internal struggles and conflicts of their students yet be able to transcend that awareness and connect with students in an authentic way to establish the trust, the open lines of communication, and the respect and authority needed to open students' minds for learning and to empower them for success. One of the fundamental ways to foster academic and personal success among students is to individualize essential parts of their learning experiences in a way that becomes meaningful, relevant, and real to them. This approach creates a trajectory to success for all students when they can realistically connect what they are learning to their real-life experiences. Another holistic and comprehensive approach is to teach students to learn for ownership.

Teaching African American Children
to Learn for Ownership

Ownership is a concept that most humans understand and is a goal that most strive to attain. Whether it is a child who claims ownership of a tangible object or an adult who holds the title deed to houses and land, the psychological effects of ownership are similarly powerful and transformative. Ownership has the regenerative power to boost the self-confidence of a child and to create pride in attainment. The resulting attitude is, "This is mine." In this instance, the kind of acquisition is less significant than the mere fact of ownership itself, which causes the child to feel a sense of executive control, exclusive possession, achievement, empowerment, accomplishment, and a higher level of self-esteem because of his ownership status. All of these outcomes validate the child and provide the basics for self-esteem building that have an effect on other areas in life.

Reflect for a moment on the dynamics that take place when children ask for a gift and the gift is received. Their reference to the item is often with the possessive adjective *my*—"This is my PlayStation, my telescope, my computer, my Barbie, my board game"—which communicates that they have begun to learn a fundamental principle associated with ownership that conveys to them certain ownership rights and privileges. Psychologically, the fact that the item belongs to them rather than to someone else is significant. The same is true for adults who refer to their acquisitions with the possessive adjective *my*. The possessive determiner *my* is empowering. It conveys to the owner the prerogative to exercise control and authority over his or her acquisition and to decide who else has access.

Could it be then that the self-esteem of children is enhanced when they own what others consider to be of value? The answer is yes. Could it be that children's self-esteem is also enhanced when they have an extraordinary talent or skill? The answer is still yes. Could it be that self-esteem and self-confidence are directly linked to success? The answer is unquestionably yes. Over the years, I have witnessed the progressive increase in self-esteem among former students as they have acquired knowledge and information in specific areas of their lives, as they developed their elocution skills, and as they perfected their crafts. These became talents, skills, and abilities that they possessed, and they realized how defining their talents, skills, and abilities were in their lives. Obviously, there is portability in the use and application of the term *ownership*. Its use transcends the reference that is often made to tangible objects to include intangible ideas and concepts; it includes talents, skills, and abilities; and, most importantly, it includes ownership of self.

Children should be persuaded that there is nothing more fundamental to success than first owning the self: who they are, what they know, what they think, what they do, what they become, how they behave, and how they interact with others. This is the kind of ownership and responsibility that children must have in their mindset: How can they perfect the person they are and the person they wish to become? That acknowledgment is the beginning of authentic ownership that lays the foundation for everything else in life. Owning behavior, ideas, principles, choices, and beliefs is essential for young people to understand. When they do not claim the ownership of their lives and their ability to transform their lives, they allow others to impose ownership claim upon them. Thus, they become subject to the whims, the wishes, and the values of others. This is the effect seen among many young African Americans whose lives have been ruined due to their association with the wrong individuals.

So, what do African American children own? Typically, what many African American children own are the negative images, the negative stereotypes, and the low self-confidence as it pertains to their lives, to their circumstances, and to their present and future conditions. They look around themselves and see squalor and despair and sometimes conclude that this condition represents them and their permanent station in life. Learning for ownership allows students to shift their thinking immediately and adopt a mindset that will lead to a productive life. This model of ownership can transform students' lives in a positive and constructive way and create a change from the perpetual status of being the victim. So, immediately, the mindset shifts from being a victim to being a master of one's fate. English poet William Ernest Henley captured this idea in his poem "Invictus" when he said, "I am the master of my fate: I am the captain of my soul" (Henley, 1875). The mindset of the victim is defensive, reactionary, aggressive, and based upon emotion whereas the mindset of the master of one's fate is confident, steady, and unconquerable. William Ernest Henley, in particular, understood the importance and the power residing in his decision to be unconquerable and undefeated. Despite his challenges, he was able to live a fulfilled life. This process, Learning for Ownership, allows the young child, the adolescent, the under-prepared child, the smart child, the latchkey child, and others to benefit from the Learning for Ownership Empowerment Model to develop an unconquerable mindset and to acquire enhanced personal net worth, increased self-esteem, and essential cognitive and academic skills to steer the course and direction of their lives.

Learning for Ownership Defined

So, what is learning for ownership? Learning for ownership is an empowerment model that renews the mindset and develops the skill sets of African American youth. It involves three components: 1) identifying and clarifying students' personal attitudinal profiles, 2) examining and validating students' experiences, thoughts and beliefs, and 3) creating an ownership culture that links entrepreneurial principles and practices to achievable goals.

PREPARING STUDENTS TO LEARN FOR OWNERSHIP

Many African American elders have, through the years, encouraged young people by saying, "You better get an education. That is something no one can take from you." Their instruction was correct, and embedded within their message was a call for ownership, for young people to acquire something that was valuable and that no one could take. Many of the African American ancestors understood the value of ownership and, through the years, acquired land and other assets that they also admonished their descendants to value and retain; for they viewed land, in particular, as a nonreplenishing commodity. They valued book learning as a gateway to freedom and independence and often said, "You had better get some book learning in your head." A learned black person was, for them, a representation of the mountaintop experience. Unlike the eighteenth, nineteenth, and parts of the twentieth centuries, education for African American children today is a gift that allows them free access to public education to increase their net worth. Thus, every day, learners can build future human, social, and economic capital by how they invest their time and by how they apply what they learn.

Regrettably, too many young African American children have not embraced the dream or recognized the value of the gift. They are dropping out of school instead of graduating from school. The task today is to reconnect children with the drive and the will to learn – not just for the sake of learning – but to learn for ownership in a way that develops gifted men and women and that sustains a prosperous nation. Now, let us begin that journey together in the chapters of this book.

Part One

Part one of this book focuses on what matters in urban education. If schools are to generate the desired outcomes from the education of African American student populations, then there are essential areas that matter: teachers matter, the philosophies of education matter, respect of students in the classrooms matters, family matters, the role of the community matters, sensitivity to sociocultural factors matters, resiliency matters, and, finally, communication matters. Part one includes a discussion of these themes and provides perspectives on proactive measures that teachers and schools can take to improve the foundational support and learning outcomes of African American children.

When educators address what really matters in public education, many of the performance issues associated with student achievement will decline. These areas that "matter" can be implemented without additional dollars in instructional support, without an additional capital campaign, and without the reengineering of schools. Developing a mandate around "what matters" for students in urban education simply requires the leadership and the will.

Teachers Matter

Teachers are heroes and heroines for individuals who have extraordinary, life-defining memories about their educational experiences; they are the villains and villainesses for those individuals who have unpleasant memories. This chapter highlights the qualities and characteristics of teachers who fall into the first category (heroes and heroines). They are the teachers who, upon reflection, bring smiles to the faces of former students when they think about the transformative power the teacher had in their lives to cause a foundational shift in their mindset. When you ask the question of them, "Who was your favorite teacher in school?" watch the expressions on the faces of former students and listen to their comments. Usually, they have nostalgic stories to tell about something the teacher did or said to make a lasting impression.

Teachers can help shape students' dreams and visions that manifest into productive lives, or they can kill the spirit and destroy hope. Figuratively speaking, teachers have the platform, the power, and the ability to speak life or death into the lives of children. Teachers who matter are transformative and speak "life" into the hearts and minds of their students. This chapter, along with the next several chapters, forms a composite of the foundational support systems needed for African American children to persist in school and to achieve success; it also creates the synergy to introduce the learning for ownership process that provides teachers with the tools to literally empower every African American child.

The focus in this chapter is on transformative teachers, those who are passionately and purposefully developing children into productive and responsible citizens and future leaders. What do transformative teachers believe and what do transformative teachers do that matter? This chapter will explain.

WHAT TRANSFORMATIVE TEACHERS BELIEVE

Transformative teachers are educators because they have the unique ability to mold, shape, and transform others; they understand their mission and purpose, so they are committed to fulfilling their calling every day of their lives. They have been transformed in their thinking and released into their purpose to educate and train. Teachers who are transformative have a belief system about children that is pure and uncorrupted. This is what they believe:

- Every child is precious.
- Every child can learn.
- Every child can succeed.
- Every child deserves respect.
- Every child deserves the teacher's best.

These are five simple beliefs that govern transformative teachers' behaviors. These beliefs and corresponding actions are filled with positive energy that lead to life-altering results in students. The corresponding actions entail behaviors that transformative teachers demonstrate to cultivate children's self-confidence and activate their motivation to learn.

WHAT ARE THE ACTIONS OF TRANSFORMATIVE TEACHERS?

Transformative teachers have a renewed mindset that is eminently fair and unbiased. They derive personal and professional satisfaction from their work to educate children and to empower them with essential knowledge and skills for a successful life. The following list delineates the actions of transformative teachers over and beyond their normal duties of creating lesson plans, writing objectives, and preparing assessments. Transformative teachers do the following:

- Transformative teachers strive to be their best selves so they can bring out the best selves in others.

- Transformative teachers motivate each child to learn.

- Transformative teachers engage students in their learning.

- Transformative teachers demonstrate flexibility and adaptability.

- Transformative teachers show the relevancy of lessons for each student.

- Transformative teachers demonstrate a commitment to each child's success.

- Transformative teachers know and call each child by name.

- Transformative teachers treat each child with dignity and respect.

- Transformative teachers introduce children to proper role models.

- Transformative teachers demonstrate proper values and morals.

- Transformative teachers vow to never give up on any child.

- Transformative teachers demonstrate a positive self-concept and expect no less from their students.

- Transformative teachers help each child to develop self-confidence and self-esteem.

- Transformative teachers encourage students to excel.

- Transformative teachers create the proper conditions for teaching and learning.

Now that you have reviewed the list of actions that transformative teachers demonstrate, those actions and the teachers' unique qualities and characteristics will be explained.

TRANSFORMATIVE TEACHERS STRIVE TO BE THEIR BEST SELVES SO THEY CAN BRING OUT THE BEST SELVES IN OTHERS

What is the best self? The best self is the self-actualized individual who is at the apex of Abraham Maslow's Hierarchy. From my observation of teachers, the best self is fully realized when teachers are able to function at optimum capacity in their skill or trade. The best self is demonstrated in the classroom preparation, in the instructional delivery, and in the interpersonal communication with students. The best self is also reflected when the teacher lives by the Golden Rule. This is particularly true of transformative teachers. They are the educators who lead by example. They are the role models of honesty, respect, common decency, integrity, competency, compassion for others, morality, and other high attributes; they seek to cultivate that same best self in others. They are adept in their subject area and fully understand their commitment to students and their purpose and mission as an educator.

TRANSFORMATIVE TEACHERS
MOTIVATE EACH CHILD TO LEARN

Transformative teachers understand how to motivate students to learn. Whether through teamwork, multimedia, or individual projects, the teachers are able to engage the students in their schoolwork in a way that inspires and motivates them. Few students enter classrooms ready to learn, but those who enroll in classes taught by transformative teachers look forward to the learning experience. The classes are always interesting, relevant, and engaging.

The question for consideration is, how does motivation occur in a classroom where students are distracted and are often grappling with serious personal problems? How can teachers refocus and motivate students to learn when there are serious personal, social, and economic challenges that affect their lives? The answer is that transformative teachers are *tuned in* to the frequency of their students. They know how to capture students' interest and motivate them to learn.

TRANSFORMATIVE TEACHERS ENGAGE
STUDENTS IN THEIR LEARNING

Student engagement creates a high level of participation among students and a high level of interest in the subject matter being taught. Students, in fact, get to learn by doing, which allows them to advance beyond the traditional lecture or rote-based learning to a higher level where they literally become involved in their learning experiences. Research data confirm that students who are engaged in their learning perform better and persist longer.

Transformative Teachers Demonstrate
Flexibility and Adaptability

Transformative teachers are astute and recognize that flexibility and adaptability are sometimes required to achieve the objectives that are set for the school day. Since transformative teachers are sensitive to the verbal and nonverbal messages that students transmit, the entire class benefits. If the teacher concludes that the planned approach for the lesson is not achieving the desired results, he is able to adapt and try other approaches that may be more effective. Since student learning is the ultimate goal, transformative teachers welcome the free flow of events that occur and make them a part of the learning experience.

Transformative Teachers Show the
Relevancy of Lessons for Each Student

Relevancy is the key to making lessons meaningful. I have heard students ask, "Why do we need to learn this material? It is dated and does not apply to us today." Transformative educators are explicit in their preparation of students for each unit by sharing the purpose, goals, learning outcomes, and relevancy of the topic to students' lives and how the outcomes may be applied. As a former television producer and host, one of the most interesting interviews that I conducted was with the late Dr. Edward Teller, the Nobel Prize-winning physicist who co-developed the atomic and hydrogen bombs. The interview was conducted at an interactive television station where hundreds of school children from throughout the region had an opportunity to participate in what was scheduled to be an hour-long interview with Dr. Teller. To my surprise, the students were genuinely involved and engaged in the conversation and asked extraordinary questions. The interview was interesting because the conversation was in lay rather than in technical, scientific terminology; the topic was relevant, and the information was understandable. The first question that I asked Dr. Teller to set the stage for the conversation was, "How is physics a part of everyday life?" Dr. Teller spoke eloquently about how physics is intricately a part of our lives. He used examples that students could relate to and understand. Immediately, he captured the students' interest and maintained a brillliant conversation for two hours instead of the one-hour interview that was initially scheduled. It was a gratifying experience to see how a subject that some thought was too technical to comprehend could be made simple, relevant, and engaging.

Relevancy can become a part of other subjects as well. Transformative teachers ensure that the objectives for the lesson show the connectedness to students' lives today.

Transformative Teachers Demonstrate a Commitment to Each Child's Success.

The job of teaching is a selfless undertaking because the focus should always be on the children. Through the teachers' actions, children know if the teacher is committed to delivering a quality education to them. In fact, the teachers' actions are quite revealing. One reason some students dismiss education as a trifling matter is simply because of the actions demonstrated by some teachers in the classroom.

Transformative teachers are committed to the students; they go over and beyond the call to duty to connect intellectually, psychologically, and relationally with each child. They see each child as a significant person instead of as a number or a seat holder for the semester or for the academic year. Therefore, the teacher who is committed to the child's success validates the child and helps the child believe in himself and in his potential. Transformative teachers are the ones who treat students civilly and fairly; they are the ones whom students respect and try very hard to please through their openness to learning and through their academic performance. In my years as an evaluator of teachers, I once saw an interesting demonstration of a transformative teacher's commitment to each child's success carried out in an elementary education classroom. The teacher wrote positive affirmations for all children in her classroom; and each day, each child would pick up the affirmation and read it to the class. One affirmation stated, "I have the ability to do all things." Another one stated, "I have greatness inside of me." Another example that I saw was a teacher who used early intervention strategies to support students who needed additional instructional and tutorial help to meet the objectives of the course. The teacher scheduled individual conferences with students to encourage those who were doing well in the class and to provide gentle support for those who were not performing well. Transformative teachers know that time spent with their students, whether twenty minutes or less, builds the tenacity and determination of the students to improve in their performance – if not for themselves – then most certainly for their teachers.

Transformative Teachers Know and Call Each Child by Name

Transformative teachers know that they validate each child's sense of self when they address them by their proper names. During the first week of school, some teachers have each child stand and introduce himself to the class and pronounce his name clearly. This is done so all children can get to know each other and learn how to pronounce their peers' names correctly. The children are also asked to tell something about themselves pertaining to a hobby, a favorite food, or favorite vacation. On the day that I visited the class, the teacher explained the purpose of the "Get to Know You" exercise. Then she, as role model, began the exercise by pronouncing her name slowly and distinctly. She described her role as teacher and her hobbies. Then, she shared information about a favorite food and a favorite vacation. After her introduction, she asked each student to do the same. Each child in the class took his turn sharing similarly. After each student's introduction, she would call the student by name and say, "Welcome to my class." The process was quite impressive. While the entire series of introductions took most of the class period to complete, it nonetheless created a bond between the teacher and the students and among the students as peers.

TRANSFORMATIVE TEACHERS TREAT EACH CHILD WITH DIGNITY AND RESPECT.

Everyone wants to be treated with dignity and respect. In fact, it costs nothing in dollars and cents to accord respect to others. In one instance that I am aware of, the teacher used titles when referring to students. So instead of calling the student John Smith by his first name, the student was called Mr. Smith. It was remarkable to see the pride that the students displayed when they were addressed by a respectable title. The effects were uplifting, particularly given that so many of the children had never heard a title used in reference to their parents, yet they were being accorded high regard. I did not follow up with the students to assess the long-term effects, but I have to believe that the use of the title caused a change in their self perception if only for a short duration of time.

TRANSFORMATIVE TEACHERS INTRODUCE CHILDREN TO PROPER ROLE MODELS

Transformative teachers understand that children are young, inexperienced, and impressionable. Thus, proper role models are essential to help the children define and shape their self image.

Children should have an opportunity to identify their role models, explain why they are role models for them, listen to them speak, observe their display of manners, evaluate how they are groomed, and assess how they interact with others. All of these factors are important.

In a program called College for Kids, I worked with the National Council of Black Women and Project GRAD to provide a six-week summer program for middle school youth. On six Saturdays, the middle school youth were transported to the campus by bus to spend four hours engaged in educational enrichment. The program was thematically based and focused on health careers, science and technology, engineering, theatre and performing arts, education, and transportation. Students had an opportunity to attend workshops that were led by accomplished and well-known professionals in each field, and they had an opportunity to network with the professionals after the presentations. At the end of the six weeks, when students were asked about their career aspirations, all of them indicated the desire to pursue one of the career fields highlighted during the summer experience. This enrichment activity was a refreshing reminder that students will aspire for more when they know what opportunities are available to them. When their sights are limited, as most of them are, their aim will be low. When their sights are broadened, I believe their aim will be raised. An introduction to proper role models in a wide array of fields can help raise the sights and the aim of the students.

Transformative Teachers Demonstrate Proper Values and Morals in Their Actions with Children

Transformative teachers are thoughtful about how they interact with others – and particularly with children. They do not want to ever be misunderstood, so they are thoughtful about their language and behavior. They believe that a person's character is defined by his actions and behaviors. Therefore, they are careful at all times to present their best selves.

Transformative Teachers Vow to Never Give Up on Any Child

Transformative teachers vow to never give up on any child, so each child's success becomes a personal commitment for them. Never giving up means that the teacher is proactive and seeks every avenue to help each child succeed. This level of commitment requires a significant investment of the teacher's time, talent, and resources, especially given that the teacher only sees the child a few hours each day and cannot insulate the child from other influences and pressures that intervene when the teacher is not present. Therefore, the transformative teacher recognizes the importance of a silent voice in the form of principles that should be instilled in children early in the learning process to build their character, to clarify their values, to enhance their self-esteem, and to sharpen their judgment.

Following is an example to show how transformative teachers made a difference in one student's life. This example is of a young African American man who recently received a YMCA award for his tenacity, scholarship, and persistency. The young man is the offspring of parents who were incarcerated. Throughout his middle and high school years, his parents spent much of their time in and out of prison. At the YMCA event, the young man made remarks about his life of overcoming challenges. He was quite eloquent and talked about the problems he faced growing up in an urban community, trying to provide for himself and his siblings after his parents were sentenced to prison. He indicated that his teachers and the president of a local organization believed in him and encouraged him. Their commitment and support helped him to believe in himself. Social service support was solicited for him and his siblings; mentors were provided to assist him. The young man was persuaded that his parents' path in life did not define him nor would it dictate his future. He graduated from high school with honors; and at the time when I met him, he was a senior at a prestigious private university and had a 4.0 grade point average. Some spectators had given up on the young man because of his parents' bad choices. Other spectators had decided his fate based upon his race and his gender. Fortunately, he was surrounded by caring teachers and community people who were transformed in their thinking and who felt it their personal responsibility to help the young man and others like him believe in themselves and in their ability to succeed.

Transformative Teachers
Demonstrate a Positive Self Concept

A positive self-concept is absolutely fundamental to success. Transformative teachers know and understand the value. The self-concept influences how a person acts, thinks, speaks, behaves, dresses, and interacts with others. Not surprisingly, the self-concept communicates volumes to others through the verbal and nonverbal messages that are transmitted.

Teachers who are transformed have positive self-concepts. They know who they are, so they are confident, self assured, and bold. These teachers are the role models that all students need, for they demonstrate the qualities and characteristics that are essential for success.

When teaching a high school African American studies class, I used a poignant essay that was written by an unnamed author that touched at the heart of the self-concept. The article was entitled, "The Slum Is Me." In essence, the author described the conditions in which he was living at the time. He talked about the environment, the social conditions, and the mindset of the people. He vividly described the slum, the housing, and the despair that consumed the people who lived there. After describing the horrific conditions, the author ended the essay by saying, "The Slum is Me." The essay was an excellent teaching tool that aroused lively discussions. Some of the students could relate to the author and felt similarly. Others were moved emotionally and blamed the victim for his condition. They thought he could physically relocate to a better environment and that would change his perception of self. Most surprisingly, other students responded with outrage. They indicated that they, too, lived in despicable surroundings but they refused to allow their surroundings to define them. They talked about why they were going to graduate, get a good job, and rescue their family members from the slum-infested conditions.

Many children in urban classrooms grow up in impoverished households; yet their self-image is not tied to the slums or to the ghettoes. Transformative teachers can help students keep the two (where they live versus who they are) separate. If they concentrate on improving upon the credentials of who they are – they can change where they live.

As we project forward to 2025, the ethnic composition of most classrooms is expected to be predominantly minority children. Many of the children will come from impoverished homes. The children should clearly understand that they are the ones who will determine their future. Society owes them nothing. They should be committed to a quality education, and they will see the difference education will make in their lives.

Transformative Teachers Help Each Child to Develop Self-Confidence and Self-Esteem

There are many ways that children can develop their self-confidence and self-esteem. Transformative teachers understand that this process is a necessary and individualized one; therefore, the transformative teachers work with the children, one-on-one, to cultivate their talents, skills, and abilities. As their competency levels develop, their self-esteem and self-confidence become stronger.

As an example, think about the persona of the star quarterback on the high school football team. Some students talk about him with pride. More importantly, he is also quite proud of his exemplary talent, his unrivaled skill, and his noted leadership. As the quarterback leads the team to more and more victories, his pride and self-confidence increase because he knows that he is quite talented and skilled at what he does. He knows that he is valued; and because of his success, he knows that others are attracted to him. When the quarterback is able to replicate his record of success, that becomes further confirmation that he is, indeed, a winner. The same is true for any student who has talent that is developed and honed; the student develops greater self-esteem and greater self-confidence.

Students who have self-confidence and a positive self-esteem believe that they can accomplish their goals. They exude the type of confidence that attracts others to them, and sometimes they attract envy. There is a story that I heard about a young man who was always told, "He thinks he's so much." While the people meant their snide remark as a criticism, he reversed it and said, "If they think that, then they must be right. I guess I am." And that mindset and confidence, coupled with hard work, catapulted him to great heights and great accomplishments.

Civic engagement activities and service learning projects are recommended for young people as a way to build their confidence and self-esteem. Service learning is also one way to prepare children for leadership roles as they engage in projects to help others. Often, it is through the circumstances of others that people in general are able to see their blessings more clearly and are able to problem-solve more objectively. It is the same with children. As they see their actions, no matter how small, helping others, this will build their self-esteem and prepare them to serve others in a larger, more responsible role.

TRANSFORMATIVE TEACHERS
ENCOURAGE STUDENTS TO EXCEL

The transformative teacher encourages students to optimize their potential. They also provide the tools and the examples for students to follow. Mediocrity is not acceptable to transformative teachers when excellence is possible. They recognize how some students settle for less when they have the potential for so much more. The so much more is what teachers who have a renewed mind see for each child. Thus, they prepare their students for excellence. I am reminded of the motto, "Excellence is the standard." The plain and ordinary usually just remains plain and ordinary. Those who embrace the mediocrity mindset usually do not ascend to great heights to achieve their maximum potential because of their low standard of expectations for themselves. Instead of looking at what is possible, they look at what has been the norm. Instead of focusing on goals that stretch them and working to achieve those goals, they find solace in criticizing others who seek to set new records and explore new frontiers.

The Chinese proverb attributed to Confucius says, "The journey of a thousand miles begins with a single step," is appropriate as you look at the march toward excellence. Similarly, the slogan, "Be all that you can be," is one used by the US Army. It touches the pulse of scaling the heights of human possibilities to achieve greatness no matter the field of endeavor. So this reflects the motivation of transformative teachers to help their students to be determined, persistent, and willing to make the short-term sacrifices in pursuit of excellence.

Transformative Teachers Create the Proper Conditions for Teaching and Learning

Creating the proper conditions for teaching and learning to occur is essential. Transformative teachers understand the importance. They create the proper conditions for students to focus on instruction and to be interactive in the teaching/learning process. The proper conditions are also essential for teachers to perform at their best.

Many years ago, in a teacher education class, my professor talked about the different types of teaching and learning styles -- one being field independent and the other being field dependent. The field-dependent students, he explained, are easily distracted by their surroundings. Therefore, the conditions for learning are essential to help maintain their attention and optimize their learning experience. Field-independent students, on the other hand, are not dependent upon their surroundings as an influencing factor in their learning. I have found over the years that the professor was correct. Setting the proper conditions for teaching and learning matter, particularly for field-dependent students – which according to some reports – includes the majority of African American students. In the end analysis, the goal is for all teachers to teach at their maximum capability and for all students to learn at their maximum potential.

No doubt, educators can also be categorized as field independent or field dependent. When I was in graduate school, I remember the confession of one of my professors. She, ironically, had been working in the public schools as a consultant to prepare student teachers to work with ethnic minority children. She, in a sidebar conversation with the class, referenced one student in particular whom she could never approach in the public school classroom because of the student's poor hygiene and general appearance. She described the student as having a snotty nose, uncombed hair, and yellow teeth. She indicated that one day she decided to make the child presentable, so she took the little girl to the restroom and cleaned her nose, combed and braided her hair, and gave her a toothbrush and paste to clean her teeth and a washcloth and soap to wash her face. After the student was groomed, the professor said, "I could finally treat her like I treated all the other students." Needless to say, I was shocked. The question for me was, How do you groom someone whose features and image you cannot change? Would that student be treated differently and suffer discrimination due to the teachers' prejudices? Obviously, there are some things that educators can change, and there are others that cannot be changed about children. Transformative teachers have a deep concern, compassion, and desire for all students to excel, and they work hard for their students despite the circumstances. More on point, transformative teachers make the students comfortable in the learning environment and remove the barriers to learning for them.

When creating the conditions for teaching and learning, transformative teachers ensure that they have the up-to-date technology, up-to-date teaching environments, current curricula, current textbooks, and ample supplemental resources for students. They are also determined to be prepared for their classes, to have appropriate credentials, and the required competencies to teach.

In all areas discussed under actions that transformative teachers perform, positive action verbs can be associated with them and their outcomes. Teachers who are transformative develop, cultivate, motivate, prepare, enhance, encourage,and promote students. Teachers who are transformative move beyond the point of thinking each child can succeed to playing an active role as a co-participant in each child's success.

CONCLUSION

Teachers' personal beliefs and actions are tipping-point influences that shape the decisions of many African American students about their persistency in school. No doubt, students who have transformative teachers have a higher persistency rate and perform better in school than students who are in classrooms where they are ignored, debased, and marginalized. The level of the teacher's view of self, coupled with his or her conviction to the teaching profession, has a direct effect on student success. In the end analysis, teachers who are transformative represent the ideal because they are committed to their profession. They are the ones who enhance student learning by equipping each student with the mindset and skill set to Learn for Ownership. So, in the end analysis, why do teachers matter? Teachers matter because they help shape the mental images that students have of themselves; they influence the aspirations that students set for themselves, and they help provide the educational foundation on which all success is based.

Philosophies of Education Matter

Teachers are always teaching and students are always learning—good, bad, or indifferent.

Dr. Asa Hilliard, 2005

The philosophy of education of the school district, the school, and of the teacher matter in the education of African American children. In 2005, I had the distinct privilege to hear Dr. Asa Hilliard, African American psychologist, historian, and Egyptologist, speak at a seminar for public school educators on the need to accelerate the cognitive development and attainment of skills among African American students. His talk was powerful and riveting. In Dr. Hilliard's 2005 address, he said that he was interested in the "methods and content of the socialization processes that we ought to have in place to create wholeness among African American people" (Hilliard, 2005). He was referring specifically to the method and content to end the intergenerational cycle of poverty and despair that seem to perpetuate thereby limiting the dreams and possibilities of African

American people. As he spoke, I thought, The wholeness that he envisions begins with the young people whose world view, values, and beliefs are in the process of being shaped. The Latin term tabula rasa describes what I mean. Tabula rasa denotes that children are born with a mental blank slate and that their knowledge and view of themselves and the world around them comes from experience and perception. Dr. Hilliard was correct, and my philosophy intersects with his perspective. There is enormous value in ensuring that the experiences that children have are wholesome, that they acquire the essential knowledge and skills needed to be competitive, and that their desire for a fruitful life is nurtured. One of Dr. Hilliard's quotes that he cited and that still resonates with me today is the following: "Teachers are always teaching, and students are always learning—good, bad, or indifferent" (Hilliard, 2005). The statement was illuminating. Educators' verbal and nonverbal behaviors are always communicating significant messages about their principles, values, and beliefs. Students hear what educators say (the verbal messages) and see what educators do (the nonverbal messages). When the two messages conflict, students are left in a quandary – wondering which of the two messages they should believe.

PHILOSOPHIES MATTER

A philosophy is a school of thought that guides a person's conduct and is grounded in beliefs, values, and behaviors. The school of thought can be influenced by a number of factors: religion, tradition, culture, stereotypes, perceptions, experiences, and history. Transformative teachers are effective because their philosophy of education guides their actions to give their best on behalf of all students.

The philosophy of education that the teacher espouses is very important. For those teachers who have not fully developed their philosophy of education, their behaviors and actions toward children could potentially be more situationally determined rather than consistent and reflective of Golden Rule principles. The philosophy of the teacher matters because it shapes and governs everything that occurs in the classroom that pertains to students. The philosophy influences how the teacher views the student, how the teacher views self, the teacher's view of the role of education, the teacher's view of the curriculum and how it is delivered, and the teacher's view of how the student should be engaged in his or her learning. Perhaps a review of great educational philosophers and their perspectives on education will help to inform the thinking for the present and help guide the pedagogical design for the future.

INFLUENTIAL PHILOSOPHERS OF EDUCATION

Two great scholars who had a significant impact upon society and the field of education during their life time were Booker T. Washington and John Dewey. Both men were great Americans who were born in the same decade. Booker T. Washington was an African American educator, author, orator, and founding president of Tuskegee Institute. He was born on April 5, 1856, into slavery on the Burroughs Tobacco Plantation in Southwestern Virginia. He had a fervor for education and, despite the institutional and social barriers, distinguished himself personally and professionally throughout the world as a renowned educator.

John Dewey was Caucasian, a philosopher, psychologist, and educational reformer. He was born on October 20, 1859 to a family of modest means in Burlington, Vermont, and distinguished himself throughout the world through his studies on civil society and education. Three calendar years separated them by birth. Unfortunately, history does not record the influence and the impact each man had on the other, but they lived during the same era, and themes within their educational philosophies are quite similar.

Booker T. Washington gained national prominence with his Atlanta Exposition Address in 1895 and, with the success of his address, he gained national prominence as a leader of African Americans. In 1901, he published his autobiography entitled *Up From Slavery*, wherein he talks about his quest to attain an education and to ultimately create an excellent postsecondary institution. Given the status of both Washington and Dewey, there is reason to believe that the post Civil War state of the nation influenced their educational philosophies. In *Up From Slavery*, Booker T. Washington highlights the enthusiasm freed slaves had for education upon receiving the Emancipation Proclamation. The description is electrifying. Washington described the actions of the people in the following manner:

> This experience of a whole race beginning to go to school for the first time, presents one of the most interesting studies that has ever occurred in connection with the development of any race. Few people who were not right in the midst of the scenes can form any exact idea of the intense desire which the people of my race showed for an education. As I stated, it was a whole race trying to go to school. Few were too young and none too old, to make the attempt to learn. As soon as any kind of teachers could be secured, not only were day-schools filled, but night schools as well. The great ambition of the older people was to try to learn to read the Bible before they died. With this end in view men and women who were fifty or seventy-five years old would be found in night-school. Some day schools were formed soon after freedom, but the principal book studied in the Sunday School was the spelling book. Day-school, night-school, Sunday-school, were always crowded, and often many had to be turned away for want of room.
>
> Washington (17)

As Booker T. Washington indicates, people flocked to school voluntarily to acquire an education. There was a strong desire among the freed slaves to read and write. Many of them, according to historical records, walked ten miles or more each day to their schoolhouses to learn.

Booker T. Washington's adult life was devoted to advancing educational opportunities for African American students at Tuskegee Normal School. He received the generous philanthropic support of donors from throughout the North and South to support Tuskegee Normal School which later became Tuskegee Institute and finally Tuskegee University. His educational philosophy encouraged practical, hands-on education in career fields and trades coupled with the opportunity to learn academic subjects. With a great trade or skill, Washington believed that the Negro in the South could make himself of enormous value, would create a demand for his services, and would, by default, elevate his economic and social status.

John Dewey's philosophy of education was grounded in the belief that education is life itself and not just preparation for life. He believed that school children should be involved in real-life tasks and challenges. In his *Pedagogic Creed*, published in January 1897, Dewey outlined specific beliefs and principles that are essential in education. He believed that the costs of academic underachievement are too high and continuously growing. Each year, students enter school with circumstances in their lives that schools are ill-prepared to accommodate. Yet, the next generation of scientists, engineers, and other skilled professionals must come from this diverse population (Dewey, 77-80). Dewey's work was published in the *School Journal* in 1897 and was released two years after Washington's Atlanta Compromise Address.

Dewey believed that much of the educational system fails because it neglects the fundamental principle of the school as a form of community life. He viewed the school as a place where certain information is to be given, where certain lessons are to be learned, or where certain habits are to be formed. Unfortunately, the value of these, according to Dewey, is conceived as lying largely in the remote future. As a result, the lessons do not become a part of the life experience of the child and so are not truly educative. Dewey believed in and promoted applied methodology for students to learn by doing. He believed that if teachers realized the dignity of their calling, the teacher would always be the true prophet of the true God and the usherer in of the true kingdom of God (Dewey, 77-80).

The educational philosophies of Booker T. Washington and John Dewey are still relevant today. Research reports reflect the attainment of skills that students learn when they engage in what Washington called *hands on* learning and what Dewey called *learning by doing* or applied methodology.

W. E. B.DuBois, was Washington's counterpart. DuBois was a sociologist, historian, and intellectual of the twentieth century. He was born in Great Barrington, Massachusetts in 1868, and broadly advocated that education must not simply teach work, it must also teach life. He addressed the need for postsecondary education to develop the most capable 10% of the black population which he referred to as the Talented Tenth. In 1888, DuBois graduated from Fisk University; and in 1895, he was the first African American to receive a Ph.D. from Harvard University. During the twentieth century, DuBois established himself as the first scholar of black life in America and believed blacks should seek higher education – particularly liberal arts instead of limiting themselves to vocational education as advocated by Washington.

As in the case of Washington, Dewey, and DuBois, other scholars have also influenced the thinking of educational practitioners. Johann Heinrich Pestalozzi and Jean Piaget are often referenced for their philosophies of education. Pestalozzi was born in Zurich, Switzerland, in 1746. His concept of education is contained in the Pestalozzi method, which emphasizes that children should learn through activity and through things, free to pursue their own interests. Jean Piaget, who contributed to the educational philosophies during the nineteenth and twentieth centuries, was also a Swiss philosopher and a natural scientist. Piaget is well known for his theory of cognitive development. He believed in the transformative powers of education and indicated that only education is capable of saving our societies from possible collapse, whether violent or gradual.

Paulo Friere, a famous Brazilian philosopher, was born on September 19, 1921, and is considered to be one of the most influential thinkers about education in the late twentieth century. He used his theories to bring literacy to the poor in third-world countries. Friere was widely known for teaching three hundred adults in Brazil to read and write in forty-five days. He believed that poor people of the world are dominated and victims of persons who possess political power. Therefore, he believed in the theory of critical pedagogy and that the oppressed must play an active role in liberating themselves. He said that the oppressed can overcome the contradiction in which they are caught only when this perception enlists them in the struggle to free themselves (Freire, 31).

Finally, another brilliant voice of the twentieth century, was Dr. Martin Luther King, Jr., who was a minister, civil rights leader, and Nobel Prize Laureate. He echoed the voices of the past in calling for equality in a broader context. He advocated for "justice to roll down like a mighty stream" for all people, irrespective of race, creed, or color. In his "I Have a Dream" speech in August 1963 on the steps of the Lincoln Memorial, he reminded America of its ideals and spoke for all children when he said, "I have a dream that my four little children will one day live in a nation where they will be judged by the content of their character and not by the color of their skin." Dr. King's philosophy called for an open educational system that provided access to all, irrespective of race, creed, or color.

All of the great thinkers and their philosophies contributed immeasurably to the field of education. Their philosophies are directly applicable to the times in which we live and provide a template that can be utilized to improve student performance in the educational system today.

ANALYSIS

The significant difference between the twenty-first century and all centuries prior to this one is the demographic profile of the population. No longer is it the white, semi-homogeneous, numerical majority that is dominating the enrollments in many urban school settings. It is now largely a growing, heterogeneous minority population that is broadly diverse. The question is, How have the philosophies of education of teachers and schools been revisited and repurposed to address the diverse educational needs of students in the twenty-first century?

While the educational philosophies of great thinkers are interesting to read to inform and inspire our thinking, it is really the educational philosophies of those on the front line in schools today that really matter. In order to serve students at the transformative level, educators should have a philosophy of education that is clear and relevant. The philosophy should take into account and address the following questions: What is the role and purpose of education in the twenty-first century? What is the role of the educator (teacher, administrator) versus the role of the student? What is the role of the school trustee? What is the role of the community and of parents in the children's education? What is the educational philosophy of the school district and/or the school? How should the teacher develop the curriculum and present it to students? What is the role of African Americans in a twenty-first century global society? What are the conditions that are necessary to facilitate learning?

No doubt, the philosophy of districts and of schools helps to influence the individual philosophies of teachers and other school personnel. In the final analysis, it is the person who has the most direct contact with the students, the teacher, who will impact their lives, "good, bad, or indifferent," for generations to come. Therefore, it is essential that the teacher's philosophy of education is student centered.

THE ROLE AND PURPOSE OF EDUCATION
IN THE TWENTY-FIRST CENTURY

In an article on twenty-first century skills, the author asked the compelling question: "What does it mean to be literate and educated in today's knowledge-based digital age?" The answer, according to the 21st Century Commission of the National Alliance of Business is that "the students need strong academic skills, thinking skills, reasoning skills, teamwork skills, and proficiency in using technology." The answer sounds very much like the messages communicated by Washington and Dewey in the nineteenth century. Dewey said, "The educational system is best when it is able to make relevant the information that students should learn, and that information should be relevant and applicable to life right now where students live, work, and play" (Dewey, 77-80). The Metiri Group indicated the following views on education for the twenty-first century.

Political, social, and economic advances in the United States during this millennium will be possible only if the intellectual potential of America's youth is developed now. It should be no surprise that what students learn—as well as how they learn it and how often they must refresh these skill sets—is changing.

So, how prepared are African American children today for life in the twenty-first century? Partial answers to the question show that there is significant work to be done. For example, in the 2007 analysis of data by the Education Trust, 30 percent of African American fourth graders could not perform at a basic level in mathematics. The reason for the abysmal results is understandable when "out-of-field" teaching is allowed in core disciplines. The Education Trust, a renowned organization whose purpose is to advance teacher quality, reported in 2009 the following: "Out-of-Field" teaching persists in key academic courses, especially in America's high poverty and high minority schools. Out-of-field teachers, as explained in the analysis of the study conducted by Richard Ingersoll, a professor at the University of Pennsylvania, are those who have neither the certification in the subject they have been assigned to teach nor the academic major in the subject area. The data show that in middle and high school mathematics, four in ten classes in high-poverty schools are taught by out-of-field teachers compared with 16.9 percent in schools serving the fewest low-income students. According to the study, in schools where there were high percentages of African American and Latino students, nearly one-third of mathematics classes are taught by out-of-field teachers compared with 15.5 percent in schools with relatively few minority students. The problem is reportedly pervasive nationwide with more than 17 percent of all core academic courses (English, math, social studies, and science) in grades 7 to 12 being taught by out-of-field teachers. In the middle grades alone, the rate jumps to 40 percent. Data from the United States Department of Education are equally alarming to see the high percentages of minority students, primarily African American and Latino, who are graduating from high schools lacking college-readiness skills. The data show that only 20 percent of African American students leave high school college ready, and 16 percent of all Hispanic students leave high school college ready. According to Dr. Jay Greene of the Manhattan Public Policy Institute, students who fail to graduate from high school prepared to attend a college or university are much less likely to gain full access to our country's economic, political, and social opportunities.

The American College Testing (ACT) officials have also tracked the lack of college readiness of students; and in their 2005 report, they highlight that only about half of the nation's ACT-tested high school students were ready for college-level reading.

So, what, in your estimation, is the problem? What do you think are the philosophies of education of teachers and school districts that produce results such as those identified in the reports? How should the problem be fixed? What is the school's philosophy of education when unqualified teachers are assigned to teach core disciplines? What does it mean when the majority of unqualified teachers are assigned to African American and Latino schools? The demands of the twenty-first century are immense; therefore, quality education for all students is of critical importance. Failing to properly educate the students will result in their either becoming a burden on society, their being minimally prepared to fill high-demand jobs, or their being relegated to a lower socio-economic status in society. If the students are not prepared in the core fields, who will become the physicians, lawyers, and educators that Dewey inquired about as early as 1897?

The national data from the United States Department of Education show that college readiness among African American and Latino students is significantly lower than it is for white high school graduates. The college-readiness rates are low and the work-readiness rates are equally low. Where is the hope and the promise of education?

ASSESSMENT OF THE ROLES OF EDUCATION

This section will allow you, the reader, to assess the role of education in your community and how well your schools are performing. Think reflectively about each question. What are the roles of education today in your community? Is a role of education to develop citizenship? Citizenship should be a fundamental part of what schools are expected to teach. Citizenship suggests that people are working to improve their communities through public service, civic engagement, volunteer work, economic participation, voluntarism, and other efforts to improve life for all citizens. Citizenship, in the context of most schools, appears to be of low priority.

How many students know about their rights as citizens? How many know about the Constitution, the Declaration of Independence, and the Bill of Rights? Students should understand their duties as citizens and their social contract made, due to their citizenship, with others. Community service and service learning are a part of citizenship activities that some schools engage in to enhance their students' involvement. These initiatives not only enhance students' involvement but they also ultimately enrich the quality of life for all.

Is preparing individuals for work or college a role of education in your community? If so, how well are your schools performing? The data show low workforce and college-readiness rates among high school graduates. The data are gloomy, with few African American children acquiring the skills necessary to be broadly competitive in the American society, much less to speak of competitiveness in a global society. The price of academic underachievement for African American children, socially, personally, and economically, is too costly. It has been documented that students who are at risk are rarely well-served by their schools, where they are tracked into substandard courses and programs holding very low expectations for their learning.

Is it the role of education to teach the morals and values of the society? How well are your schools performing in this instance? Are schools teaching students socialization skills, and to what effect? Data show the high incidence of moral decline among some youth as demonstrated in their inappropriate behavior and conduct.

Is it the role of education to prepare students for global citizenship? Are educational institutions teaching children the global consciousness needed to be full participants in the decisions about human rights, ecological sustainability, homelessness, hunger, and unattended health problems? Global citizenship is knowledge about and participation in a world community where students can apply their skills to help solve problems that threaten the larger society. How well are your schools performing this role?

Is it the role of education to accelerate the academic and career pathways for students who will enter the workplace or who will enroll in college immediately upon high school graduation? Dale Parnell, author of *The Neglected Majority*, remains accurate in his assessment that there is need for concern about the 75 percent of students who will not graduate. Dr. Parnell, former public school teacher, principal, superintendent, and community college president believed that it is a waste of the nation's resources and a national embarrassment and a threat to the country that so many students do not complete an education. Tech Prep Associates Degree is one plan supported by Dr. Parnell that seeks to provide a career pathway for students. Dual credit does the same. Through Dual Credit, students are able to earn credentials that accelerate their access to a job or their transfer to a four-year postsecondary institution upon completion of their high school diploma. My observations suggest that K-12 educational institutions, some of which are performing at exemplary levels, need to conduct a complete audit of their practices and policies. Secondarily, they should refocus their efforts on the philosophy by which they will operate, bring clarity to the role and purpose of education at their schools, then execute their responsibilities with a higher level of integrity for the students whom they serve.

The Philosophy of School Districts

Many public school districts and their schools have mission statements and philosophies that guide their educational practices and their instructional programs. The philosophy of education for the district helps focus all teachers and administrators on the role and purpose of education and how students should be served. The value of education cannot be overstated. Booker T. Washington and John Dewey knew it, and so did all philosophers who either came before or after them. No matter the economic status or the prior conditions, African American children can learn and will learn if they are taught by transformative teachers and guided by educational philosophies that are focused on student success.

Respect of Students in the Classroom Matters

"How are you, Mr. Smith?" the teacher asked the student.

"I am fine, Mrs. Jones. How are you today?" the student replied.

This does not sound like a typical exchange between a teacher and a student in most situations that we are familiar with in day-to-day encounters. The more typical greeting is the following.

"Good morning," says the teacher.

"Good morning," replies the student.

In this instance, both parties acknowledge that the other is visible and that they exist. In the next exchange, where the teacher says, "Good morning, Bill," and the student replies, "Good morning, Mrs. Jones," the message is clear that Mrs. Jones is in authority and is accorded a courteous respect by Bill. Finally, when the teacher consistently walks past Bill and never acknowledges him, that behavior might suggest what Ralph Ellison refers to as an invisible man experience. Ralph Ellison describes the effects of invisibility in his book entitled *Invisible Man* which will be discussed in more detail in a later chapter on Teaching African American Student Populations. He says,

"I am invisible, understand, simply because people refuse to see me" (Ellison, 7). Why do people refuse to see him? Is it really because of the color of his skin? In most situations the lack of acknowledgment would signal a lack of courteous regard for Bill. But is Bill being overly sensitive and reacting to sociocultural conditioning? What is truth in this instance?

Respect as illustrated in the use of the social title is a very important example of courteous regard in the African American community. For many, the social title represents a badge of distinction. What affect do you think the use of social titles would have on African American student performance, persistence, and completion if it were used on a regular basis? I suspect that teachers would see a different attitude demonstrated among African American children.

It has always been the expectation that children must show respect for their elders in general and for teachers in particular. Being respectful, in this instance, is communicated one way only -- from the student to the teacher. So, in the end analysis, some children believe, "If I show you courteous regard, then you should show me courteous regard in return. If you do not respect me, then I will not respect you." This attitude is prevalent among students in many of the classroom dynamics across the country.

THE IMPORTANCE OF RESPECT

Respect is required in any relationship and is the minimal expectation that anyone should have of others in interpersonal situations. The show of respect is particularly important in teaching and learning situations for a variety of reasons. First and foremost, individuals, no matter the age, resist contact with people who disrespect them. The natural response is to retreat. Secondly, people usually rise to the level of expectations that others in authority have of them. If the teacher expects the children to misbehave or to perform poorly, then the students will likely respond accordingly. If the teacher expects the children to behave mannerly, then the students will likely fulfill that expectation also. Respect for self and for others is essential and helps establish the foundation for good interpersonal relationships, whether personal or professional. "Courteous regard" is the working definition used in describing the respect that a person should display. This is rather simple, but it is unconventional thinking for some to accord respect to children. This chapter focuses on the dynamics that occur in teaching and learning situations when students are treated with respect.

RESPECT FOR STUDENTS

I have often thought there should be a bill of educational rights for students. Too often, African American children in particular are treated disrespectfully. They are often thought of as uneducable and are often treated that way. Teachers who respect their students usually have a profound effect on their lives. In addition to the positive effect of their teaching, they demonstrate authentic compassion, guidance, and moral support as needed. Students, on the other hand, never want to disappoint the teachers who believe in them. It is remarkable how many testimonials I have heard over the years about students who excelled because their teachers encouraged them, respected them as individuals, and held high expectations for them. In an environment of respect and trust, the successful teachers cultivate students' belief systems that convince them that they can succeed and accomplish their goals, despite their circumstances.

Respect is more than a verbal expression. It is more than telling someone that you have courteous regard for them or telling someone that you are committed to their success and their best interests. Respect is also a verb that requires action through the demonstration of behaviors, the projection of attitudes, and the energizing affect of beliefs that can help to empower and uplift students.

RESPECT MATTERS

Self-respect as well as respect for others is essential. The adage is true, "How can you expect someone to respect you if you don't respect yourself?" Think about the person who conducts himself in a disrespectful manner or who dresses inappropriately. Consider the person who is loud, uses profanity, or has loose morals. Do you automatically accord respect to those individuals, or do you respectfully avoid them? Following is a list of behaviors that should trigger caution for practitioners to avoid the allegations of disrespect.

- Greetings: How do you greet African American children? The use of slang or familiar expressions with people you do not know in an effort to fit in or be accepted can be offensive.

- Volume and Tone of Voice: What is the volume and tone of your voice when talking to African American children? Do you raise the volume in order to be heard? Do you speak slower because you think you will be better understood? Do you use a different tone because you see African Americans as being inferior?

- Use of Social Titles: Do you avoid using social titles with African Americans? Why? Do you use the first name with African Americans more than you do with other ethnic groups?

- Cultural References: Do you feel a need to qualify your lack of bias by indicating that you have many African American friends, or do you indicate to those that you think are extraordinary that they are different from the rest?

- Dress: Do you try to dress in ethnic attire to give the appearance of kinship or of acceptance? If the attire is worn for these reasons, then the motivation is wrong.

- Nonverbal Gestures and Expressions: Does your body language differ from your verbal expressions? Does your body language communicate negative messages through the use of your gestures, body posture, or spatial distance?

- Eye Contact: Do you only have eye contact with people whom you view as your equal?

- Spatial Distance: What is the distance that usually separates you when talking to African American people? Is that distance significantly different from the space between you and other ethnic groups?

It is always better to demonstrate authentic respect rather than attempting to curry favor, which is often viewed as disingenuous and disrespectful.

CULTIVATING RESPECT

There are ways to increase respect for others. The best way to develop respect for another is through personal conversations and shared-meaning experiences. The shared meaning is often the result of one-on-one conversations where people learn about their similar likes, dislikes, and personal journeys. Cultivating respect is an everyday opportunity. When meeting people for the first time, there is an opportunity for polite conversation about who they are, where they were born, their hobbies, their views on various social issues, and their values, likes, dislikes, and perspectives on life. Sometimes, people do not fully self-disclose; nevertheless, the conversations lend themselves to opportunities for people to form opinions and impressions. The conversations can lead to closer alliances and a sense of shared values, or the opposite might occur. Nevertheless, there is a decision point that can be reached based upon a conversation with the person to understand his world. That same type of polite "get to know you" conversation seldom occurs with students. Often, students are known rather superficially unless there are compelling reasons, such as disciplinary problems, that necessitate more detailed conversations with them.

GETTING TO KNOW AND RESPECT STUDENTS
THROUGH THEIR PERSONAL STORIES

Personal stories usually have the power to connect people in meaningful ways. Without infringing upon the personal lives of students, it is important to allow them to engage in stream-of-consciousness writing to put on paper what is on their minds. Often the written word helps students clarify their thoughts and their feelings. In addition to stream-of-consciousness writing, journaling is another, more focused way, to help students record their experiences and use their journals as a tool for personal reflection and to record their daily thoughts.

The personal stories can be written in the journal or spoken and are usually shared around a common theme that all students can discuss in class. For example, students can write about their career aspirations or their *rags to riches journey* and openly discuss future aspirations and what will be required to achieve their goals. As students share their dreams and aspirations, other students will become motivated and bonds will be formed among students who have similar interests.

The personal stories are important for African American children because seldom are there opportunities for many of them to talk with others about their ambitions and to get feedback and encouragement.

JASON'S STORY

This example highlights Jason's story and explains why encouragement, support, and respect are important. Jason was a young man with great potential, yet he dropped out of school due to a perceived lack of respect from his family and friends. He grew up in a single-parent home on the proverbial wrong side of the tracks. His physical features were different from his siblings and even from the other children in the community. He was light-skinned; they were all dark. Jason had straight hair; theirs was curly. Jason had aquiline features; theirs were more prominent. Jason was tall, and they were short. Jason made excellent grades. He was teased by his siblings because of his physical differences and taunted by his peers because of his academic performance. Because of his desire to fit in and be accepted, he overcompensated. Gradually, Jason began to change: he began to speak slang talk; he began to dress differently; he began to walk differently; and he began to, on occasion, strike out at his peers. Despite the fact that Jason was doing well in school academically, he dropped out in the tenth grade and never returned. When asked why he dropped out, Jason said that he could not take the pressure; neither did he want to continue to isolate his family and friends, many of whom had dropped out of school and were living mediocre lives. He did not fit in with black students or white students. Jason took the easy way out and dropped out.

Respect from others and acceptance by others are real issues for many children, particularly among young men. The Bowen Theory of human functioning addresses the impact of relationships. Two of the eight concepts of the Bowen Theory resonated with me: the multi-generational transmission process and the differentiation of the self. The multi-generational transmission process is one that describes how small differences in family relationships during childhood and adolescence determine how much self the child develops. Once established, the level of self, according to the Bowen Theory, rarely changes. Thus, everything in life is affected—including educational accomplishments—by how much self a person develops in childhood (thebowencenter.org).

How could the level of self affect educational accomplishments? The effect can be seen on a regular basis among children who have low self esteem and among children who have not been taught to think critically. An additional question is, how does a child aspire for success when there is the fear that success will alienate him from family and friends? It is unfortunate when people resign themselves to mediocrity in order to maintain relationships, but this codependency with others is real and shows how relationships are affected and how aspirations are influenced by others. In the end analysis, the words people speak have power to create exactly what people say. For students whose self-image and self-confidence are marginal, they are more dependent upon positive input from others to help shape their identities; therefore, what is said and how it is said are critically important to them. Other students have developed a mental *kill switch* that overrides anything that differs from their view of self. Irrespective of the child's level of self-confidence, it is important that all students be encouraged and accorded proper respect.

Situations That Cause Loss of Respect

Self-control is vital in all instances. One thing that I have observed in working with groups over the years is that people who control their emotions, their temperament, and their disposition fare better than those who are always losing control and being confrontational. Could Jason have learned early on to subdue his inclination to strike out either in self-defense or as an instigator and to find a different way to solve confrontations? I remember countless examples where my opinion of people changed dramatically based upon how they handled tough situations. When I say tough situations, I am referring to those emotionally-charged moments where either a person was being undermined, ridiculed, embarrassed, or challenged in a fierce way. Those who were able to maintain their disposition, their calm, and their dignity and responded in an unemotional, intelligent way were the most impressive to me. Unfortunately, mastering emotions is not an art; it is a skill that must be learned and developed by both teachers and students. Think of the countless numbers of individuals who respond emotionally only to regret their outbursts or their lack of decorum. I am confident that many people who attend anger management classes could have benefitted from a lesson or two in advance on how to manage their emotions. The same is true for people who are incarcerated for rash actions triggered by their uncontrolled emotions. While emotional intelligence tests have been challenged by some scholars as having questionable predictive value, there are, nonetheless, many scholars who champion the concept of emotional intelligence and its importance. Unlike the traditional definitions of intelligence that, for years, measured cognitive aspects of problem solving and memory, the emotional intelligence quotient describes an ability, capacity, or skill to perceive, assess, and manage the emotions of one's self, of others, and of groups.

In the early 1920s, E. L. Thorndike was one of the trailblazers in the conversation regarding multi-intelligences. At that time, he described the skill of understanding and managing other people as social intelligence. Through research, some scholars have determined that traditional definitions of intelligence do not fully explain performance outcomes. Therefore, the quest for a broader view of intelligence has gained popularity. The most common definition of emotional intelligence, as defined by persons in the field, is, "The ability to perceive emotions, integrate emotion to facilitate thought, understand emotions, and regulate emotions to promote personal growth" (Thorndike, 227-235). This construct suggests that emotionally-intelligent people should be able to perceive emotions, use emotions, understand emotions, and manage emotions. In the book entitled *Working with Emotional Intelligence*, Daniel Goleman explored the function of emotional intelligence and indicated that emotional intelligence is a strong predictor of success.

In my estimation, everyone should develop and, where appropriate, sharpen their emotional intelligence. As indicated earlier, a lack of emotional intelligence can damage good relationships, irrespective of whether the responses are displayed in the classroom, in a working relationship, in a family, or on the playground. Often, the responses can lead to heightened conflict and physical altercations or even total separation from people. Similarly, emotional-intelligent responses and an appropriate display of behaviors can achieve a positive end result like creating an inseparable bond between and among individuals.

So, what is intelligent behavior? Intelligent behavior is a preferred, learned response irrespective of the person, place, thing, or circumstance. In some venues, it is called home training. It used to be that home training covered the gambit on how to treat people, what to say, and what is considered an inappropriate response and why. Training to be more responsible as an emotionally-intelligent individual can be a transformative process and is highly recommended. The cumulative effects of each person's training can be a benefit to the larger society and certainly to the success of African American students.

Effects of Respect in the Classroom

A culture based upon respect provides a platform for everyone to be valued, everyone's voice to be heard, and everyone to feel empowered. Teachers in educational classrooms throughout the country can begin to set the standard for respect by creating rules of engagement that will be used to interact with others. It is never too early for school children to learn the importance of respecting themselves, respecting others,and respecting property – whether theirs or someone elses.

In conclusion, as we saw in Jason's story, respect is vital and is the conduit through which effective teaching, optimum student learning, and ultimate student success can occur.

Parents and Family Matter

This chapter discusses the important role that parents and extended family members play in the lives of African American children. To frame the discussion, information is provided from US Census Bureau data that shows the demographics of African Americans in key defining areas such as marriage and family, educational attainment, and employment. The data are utilized as a springboard to present actions that parents and extended family members can take to build the self esteem of their children and actions that school districts can take to prepare more families for student advocacy.

In examining the data, it is apparent that the immediate family structure within the African American community is weakened due to a variety of factors. According to the US Census data, there were 33.8 percent married couple families in the African American community in 2008 versus 53.4 percent of married couple families of all races. Among the single parents, 29 percent of households were headed by African American females with no husband present versus 12.5 percent among all races. The data also showed that the female householder raising children under eighteen years of age, but with no husband present, at 17.8 percent for Black households versus 7.4 percent for all races.

Perhaps you would agree that the family structure, which is considered the bedrock of civilization, is tenuous for many children. The family constitutes the unit that teaches the youth about the cultural traditions, values, and beliefs. In many cultures, the family has been the refuge where children could be nurtured and raised with a formidable confidence in themselves. How can that confidence be developed among African American children whose immediate family support systems are also weak and, in some instances, broken? Who is there to fill the void when the immediate family is incapable? How can children develop the confidence they need when they are told they are no good and that everyone in their line of foreparents is no good as well? Hearing demeaning comments from others outside the family creates one set of perceptual issues. Hearing the negative comments from inside the family creates another set of perceptual issues and causes self-doubt, shame, and, sometimes, self-hatred. The voices of family members can be instrumental in helping to mould and shape the children's present and future. The words that are spoken to children have extraordinary power and influence. The first words that convey the essence of who the child is and what the child becomes should be affirming and spoken by the people closest to them: the parents and family members. So, in those families where the parents are incapable of fulfilling their duties and responsibilities to their children, it becomes the responsibility of the extended family to stand in the gap for the sake of the children.

DEMOGRAPHICS ON AFRICAN AMERICANS

The demographics on African Americans illustrate why there is such a deepening crisis within the African American community and shows why the toll is so great on many African American children. According to US Census data, there were 308.4 million Americans in 2008; African Americans comprised 41.1 million (13.5 percent) of the total US population. African American males comprised 48 percent of the black population while African American females comprised 52 percent. Of the African American males between the ages of thirty and thirty-four, the Census data indicate that this group has the highest incarceration rate of any race or ethnic group in the United States. Additionally, of the entire male inmate population—which is reflected as being 2.1 million male inmates in jail or prison—black males represent the highest percentage: 35.4 percent black, 32.9 percent white, and 17.9 percent Hispanic. Over one third of the males in jail or prison are between the ages of twenty and twenty-nine.

Educationally, in 2008, according to Census data, 81 percent of African Americans age twenty-five and over have at least a high school diploma. The data also showed that 1.4 million African Americans twenty-five and older have an advanced degree. The college enrollment was 3.2 million blacks, representing an increase of roughly 2 million from seventeen years previously. Finally, in the area of educational attainment, 18 percent of African Americans twenty-five and older have a bachelor's degree or more.

In the area of employment, the African American unemployment rate is almost double that of the overall population. In 2009, the rate of unemployment for African Americans was 7.5 percent versus 4.2 percent overall. The poverty rate among African Americans in 2009 was 25.8 percent. For African American mothers who were single, 41 percent lived in poverty compared to 7 percent of married couple African American families. The predominant areas of employment for African Americans was in educational services, health care, social assistance, and retail jobs. In the area of housing, the data show that more African Americans rent than own their homes; and finally, in the area of transportation, 20 percent of African Americans did not own an automobile at all while 91 percent of all other Americans owned a vehicle.

In examining the critical data, it is evident that the low level of education, the absence of a parent from the home, the low-level skills, and socio-economic status have an effect on the quality of life of African American families and the opportunities and foundational support for the children. Poverty is the condition that results when limited education and limited skills trap persons into a low level of existence. Therefore, a broader net of support must be cast and new methodologies must be used to ensure that African American children benefit from and succeed in the educational system.

FAMILY INVOLVEMENT IN EDUCATION

The broader net of support for African American children includes the extended family. The united strength of the extended family helps create greater accountability for the children, a broader platform of support for the children, and a unified voice that the children are hearing about the expectations being held for them. Often, as reflected in the data, the children's parents are not available to support them due to a variety of factors: incarceration, divorce, or other circumstances. Those circumstances represent just a few reasons why the extended family is so critically important for the sake of the children and for the sake of our collective future. In fact, in many African American families, the grandmother, aunt, or some other family member raises the children anyway and assumes total responsibility for the oversight, growth, and development of the children. No matter who is the primary guardian, there are some essential actions that guardians can take to empower the children who are in their care. Twelve of the most critical actions other than the normal duties of feeding, clothing, sheltering, and protecting them are provided below.

Essential Action One: Communicate Positive, Esteem-Building Messages

No matter the guardian's level of education or whether one or both parents are in the home, the verbal messages that are communicated to children help define them and shape their attitudes and behaviors. Messages that encourage and support are easy to learn and easy to say. There should be messages that undergird, build, lift, and support. Examples of contrasting messages that are frequently used are provided below. Obviously, the negative messages are destructive and should never be communicated.

CONTRASTING MESSAGES

Positive Messages	Negative Messages
I love you.	I hate you.
You are a blessing to me.	You are a burden to me.
You are intelligent.	You are dumb.
You have a beautiful spirit	You have a demon inside you.
You will be successful	You will never amount to anything.
You will be an executive one day.	You are no good.
You have value.	There's nothing to you.
You have a fine personality.	You get on my nerves.
You are courageous.	You are a scary cat.
You are a winner.	You are a loser.
You are beautiful.	You are so ugly.
You make me proud.	You are an embarassment.
You have great potential.	You have limited ability.

The list of contrasting messages can continue *ad infinitum*; however, the distinction is clear. One set of statements can lift and build a child's self-esteem, and another set of statements can have the opposite effect. What effect do you think the negative messages have on children?

Now, consider also the playground banter and its effect. Friends also have the responsibility of supporting and uplifting each other. That is why they are friends. Language such as *dawg* and other negative or pejorative terms used on the playground are not terms of endearment. What could possibly be endearing about the dehumanization of anyone, particularly a friend or family member? Instead, words that have positive denotations and that are character defining are preferred. Given the brilliant, creative minds of youth on the playgrounds of America and their abilities to rap, to play ball, to dance, to create new rhymes and rhythms, it is worthwhile to challenge them to develop a nomenclature that replaces the current, negative playground banter with positive language that is affirming, endearing, and also *"cool."*

Essential Action Two: Help Children Believe in Themselves

This act is probably one of the most important gifts that anyone can give to another: helping them believe in their ability, their voice, their skills, their talents, and in themselves. This belief is communicated through the verbal acknowledgment that children receive from those around them. For every act, whether large or small, the compliments and verbal support that others freely give cause children to become more confident and believe in themselves.

Essential Action Three: Encourage Children to Read

I remember the slogan from years ago that said, "Reading is Fundamental." That was a true statement then and is proven to be true today. Family members can encourage the children to read.

If the parents or other guardians are illiterate, their children can improve upon their skills and abilities by reading to them. If the family cannot afford to purchase books, periodic trips to the public libraries provide an avenue to a whole new world of learning resources for them.

Essential Action Four: Engage the Children in Meaningful Conversations

Parents and family members should regularly engage their children in meaningful conversations about their schoolwork, what they are reading, how they are feeling, the events of their day, their aspirations, and current events. The conversation should not always be limited to the time when there is a problem to be addressed or when the child has been mistreated by someone. The conversation helps strengthen the child's social interaction and conversational skills.

Essential Action Five: Support Children's Educational Involvement

Every attempt should be made to support the child through attendance at events and activities that the child participates in at school. The attendance communicates to the child that he is special, he is valued, and he is supported by his family. It also communicates that the child is not alone, so it helps create the feeling of emotional and psychological security that the child needs.

Essential Action Six: Teach Children Responsibility

Everything that the child learns early in life, he learns from his parents or those closest to him. Do the family members go to work? Do they have a steady job? Do they hold the child responsible to perform certain chores? Does the child attend school regularly? Is the child punctual and prepared for school at all times? Parents, guardians, and other family members can help create responsible children who will, hopefully, become responsible adults.

Essential Action Seven: Help Children Shape Their Image

People make judgments about individuals based upon the way they speak, the way they dress, and the way they make them feel. The way they dress is not dependent upon expensive, tailormade clothing. Instead, it is evaluated by cleanliness, pressed instead of wrinkled attire, and overall grooming. Some children see their family members leave home in hair rollers, pajamas, house slippers, pants sagging, face unwashed, hair uncombed or unbrushed. Such lack of concern about the self-image leads to a show of disrespect to them from others. It is important to impress upon the children to put their best foot forward at all times because the first impression that others get of them is the one that lasts.

Essential Action Eight: Indulge Children in Acting Out Their Dreams

The children might have a desire to act out their dreams by pretending to be a scientist, an attorney, a nurse, a teacher, or a preacher. Whatever the constructive dream, the parents or guardians should be patient and encourage the children. Sometimes by just listening to them or watching them dramatize how they will walk, talk, or dress in certain situations deepens the child's desire to fulfill his dream. At the end of their dramatization, the parents or guardians can further encourage the child to let him know that they are excited about the child's present and what the child will become in the future. I am reminded of a young boy who lived across the street from my family. He was no more than six years old and on a regular basis, he would set up his tomato crate in front of their house and use it as his pulpit as he pretended to preach for five or ten minutes at a time. The young boy grew up, and in fact, became an ordained minister of a church that he still pastors. I have not heard him preach as an adult, but from hearing him as a child, I would imagine that he is one of the fire and brimstone preachers.

Essential Action Nine: Let the Child Know That You Love Him or Her

One of the most comforting feelings is knowing that you have someone who loves you and that you can rely upon in the time of need. Some families express their affection easily. Others are more stoic. In fact, some adults have commented that their parents never told them that they loved them; they never embraced them, so they similarly grew up thinking that they should not express affection or show emotions toward others. It is validating for children to hear a parent say how proud the parent is of them and how much the parent loves them. The verbal expression of love creates a special bond among loved ones.

Essential Action Ten: Be a Role Model of Ethics, Values, and Principles

Children need to see parents and family members doing the right thing. If parents and other family members are not proper role models of ethics, values, and principles, it should not be a surprise when children do not have and do not display those ethical values and principles. Children learn first in the home, and the home should set the example of good behavior.

Essential Action Eleven: Help Children Develop a Thirst for Learning

Parents can help children sharpen their skills in mathematics and in writing by getting them to help with the family budget, participating in grocery shopping, and helping to write letters of correspondence to others. Involvement in family matters that pertain to math and English will help develop the children's skill sets in both areas.

Essential Action Twelve: Teach Children the
Importance of Time Management

As a part of teaching children how to be responsible, they should also be taught how to manage their time wisely. Effective time management is essential for them to learn to avoid procrastination. Time management allows them to schedule time for everything they need to do and to reserve time for the things they want to do.

Preparing Families for Mentorship

Educational institutions have a great resource at their disposal. That resource consists of parents and other family members to assist the school in productive ways to help accomplish the goals of student persistency and success. The most effective way to connect the parents as a liaison to the school is to make them an advocacy partner and give them an action plan that they can work to accomplish in conjunction with the schools. One way to involve the parents/guardians is through the Learning for Ownership A-Z Support List.

The Learning for Ownership A-Z Support List is really fundamental. It does not cost anything. It requires personal time from the parents and family members and vision and foresight from the school administration. To begin the process, a parent/guardian orientation session is recommended to discuss the Learning for Ownership A-Z List of prompts and explain how the list can be used in conjunction with the school on a twenty-six week basis before new prompts are provided to them. The level of educational attainment of parents or guardians is not a factor in their ability to perform the advocacy work in conjunction with the school. Commitment from them is the key. During the orientation, each word on the list should be explained to the family member, followed by examples showing how the family member can operationalize the word to achieve the goal in support of their children. During the twenty-six-week period, the parents/guardians are asked to keep a journal of their experiences and of their children's improvement. If keeping a journal is a problem for some parents/guardians who perhaps cannot read and write, they should simply recall the high and low points of the twenty-six-week journey to communicate their oral feedback at parent and teacher meetings.

Following is the Learning for Ownership A-Z List for the first twenty-six weeks of the school year.

- Week 1: A=Accord refers to the agreement that the school, the teacher, and the parent or family member make to work harmoniously as advocates for their children's success.

- Week 2: B=Bolster refers to the actions of the parents to reinforce the messages of the school and to simultaneously build up and boost the morale of the child.

- Week 3: C=Counsel refers to the actions of the parents to advise the child pertaining to the expectations of the school.

- Week 4: D=Develop refers to the actions of the parents to promote the growth and development of the child intellectually, socially, educationally, and recreationally.

- Week 5: E=Empower refers to the actions of the parents to enable children to assume responsibility, to exercise ethical values, and to exercise their critical thinking skills to make good choices.

- Week 6: F=Fair-minded refers to the actions of the parents to enable children to make unprejudiced decisions about issues, people, and circumstances.

- Week 7: G=Gratitude refers to the actions of the parents to teach children to be thankful and appreciative and the need to express their gratitude after each kind or thoughtful act shown toward them.

- Week 8: H=Help refers to the actions of the parents to teach the child how to both give assistance to others and how to graciously receive assistance from others.

- Week 9: I=Indweller refers to the actions of the parents to teach children about the power of their inner-activating spirit.

- Week 10: J=Justice refers to the actions of the parents to teach children right action in all instances.

- Week 11: K=Kind refers to the actions of the parents to help their children have a sympathetic nature and to be loving and gentle to others.

- Week 12: L=Love refers to the actions of the parents to teach their children to show tenderness and devotion.

- Week 13: M=Model refers to the actions of the parents to teach children to display appropriate behavior at all times, as they are role models for younger children.

- Week 14: N=Nimble refers to the actions of the parents to teach their children to be flexible and adaptable.

- Week 15: O=Ownership refers to the actions of the parents to teach their children the importance of striving for ownership in all aspects of their lives.

- Week 16: P=Protect refers to the actions of the parents to teach their children to protect themselves from attacks, physically and mentally.

- Week 17: Q=Quality refers to the actions of the parents to teach their children that everything they do should be exemplary and reflect quality.

- Week 18: R=Respect refers to the actions of the parents to teach children to have a high regard for themselves and consideration for others.

- Week 19: S=Self Esteem refers to the actions of the parents to teach children to value themselves and to identify ways to enhance their self image and their self esteem.

- Week 20: T=Think refers to the actions of the parents to prepare their children to engage in higher-order thinking at all times.

- Week 21: U=United refers to the actions of the parents to teach their children that it is important to be connected to those with whom they are in agreement or with whom they share similar values.

- Week 22: V=Validate refers to the actions of the parents to help students reaffirm their self-worth and value.

- Week 23: W=Winner refers to the actions of the parents to instill the victorious spirit in children.

- Week 24: X=X refers to the actions of the parents to help children obliterate or wipe out their past deficiencies and to replace their old thoughts with productive, success-oriented thoughts.

- Week 25: Y=Yahweh refers to the actions of the parents to teach their children to be positive, affirmative yea-sayers and confident in themselves and in the power that resides within them.

- Week 26: Z=Zealous refers to the actions of the parents to instill in their children the passion to pursue their interests with fervor.

CONCLUSION

Obviously, the family matters in all things pertaining to the early stages of child development. What do the children hear, see, touch, experience, taste—those are the things that will affect their psyches and ultimately shape their mindsets. No doubt, raising children is very important work that requires more than one dedicated person in the family to adequately perform the job. Raising children must be a 100 percent total commitment. Therefore, people who make the decision to have a child should be prepared for a long-term joint venture (about twenty-one years) and the allocation of time required to properly raise the child to adulthood.

In my early years as a university professor, a colleague whose specialty was interpersonal relationships often made the statement, "Romance without finance is ignorance." I thought the expression was rather ridiculous until I began to see the results. The results are the repeated cycles of poverty, the staggering rate of unemployment, the low educational attainment levels, the low-income jobs, and the high incarceration rates. The problems will persist until children recognize the value in completing an education that leads to a livable income for themselves and for their family.

Finally, someone must command the attention of the children and redirect their lives. It could be that the collective voices of African American families to their children in partnership with the schools could be the catalyst that captures their attention, renews their minds, and ultimately makes the difference.

The Role of the Community Matters

Community engagement is a vital component to school success. This chapter explores the use of grass-roots initiatives to engage the community in support of educational excellence and equity for African American children.

Community engagement is an inclusive and interactive process of involvement. It provides the community with access to essential information and the schools with a viable network of advisory support. The ultimate benefit is to create a better-educated community and to create an enhanced quality of life for the residents. This support network is particularly important for public schools due to the vast resources that are needed and that the community can provide.

For several years, I served as a community organization specialist for a local agency. At that time, I learned the importance of grassroots efforts in rallying the community to support causes that would impact their lives. The core components to effective community engagement were providing essential information about the issues, facilitating discussions to arrive at recommendations, and providing resources to assist in community action. As a young professional in my early twenties, equipped with a college degree in hand, my first priority was to know the issues and to know the pros and cons associated with the issues before convening small groups of community persons to engage them in discussions. I worked with agency personnel to send out letters and memoranda to community groups to invite them to meetings, and I asked to be on the agendas of various community organizations to briefly discuss their community, the problems that existed, how they could potentially address the problems, and to answer questions. It was a very productive and effective process. I found that talking to individuals was easy and generating their support only required telling them how they would be affected if change did not occur. Now, as a college president aware of the prevailing problems that confront many African American children in the educational system, it is evident that there is the need for community engagement as the best vehicle to help address and correct the problem of the failing schools that are failing ethnic minority children. My focus in this work is on African American children in particular since most of my early work in the public school system and in community engagement initiatives focused on African American populations. While I feel certain that the same issues abound in other ethnic minority communities, I have not yet conducted the extensive research to confirm my hypothesis. Additionally, I want to avoid generalizing or painting all ethnic minorities with a broad brush just as I have been careful to avoid that approach with African Americans. No doubt though, it is time for a focused effort to arouse the consciousness within the broader community about the problems within the educational system and to provide community leaders with practical approaches to help resolve problems that exist. Everyone has heard the abridged version of the problems. Also, many individuals who are well-intentioned and who want to improve education for all students are provided very limited information; therefore, their effectiveness is curtailed. Those persons who take a stand independently are often viewed as agitators, troublemakers, and detractors.

Armed with limited information, community partners are left with the sound bites and press clippings of what is happening in their schools without the substantive information needed to support a revolution in public school education. To avoid the embarrassment and appearance of incompetence, capable community leaders redirect their limited time for community service to other areas that are less controversial and conclude that the trained professionals and school trustees will do the right thing and make the right decisions. That assumption is true in many instances, but there are also instances where trustees get only the sound bites of information, so they are also limited in their ability to make all of the right decisions in a timely manner. Very simply, too many children are graduating from high school lacking college-readiness skills. The majority of freshmen-level students at colleges and universities are in need of developmental education and remedial support before they can begin their academic degree plans. While the community elects trustees to be their voices on school boards, that structure still needs the support and input of the broader community, so that is why community involvement matters.

What the Public Needs to Know

What are the success and failure rates of students in the local public schools? Parent-Teacher Organizations (PTOs) are actively involved and ask the critical questions, but how much pressure is applied to the school administrators and their boards to ensure accountability? I recall when I was working on a new initiative called "The Dual Credit Plan" (Fincher-Ford), I partnered with a young man who was an assistant superintendent of schools. He knew that the bureaucracy would not move to adopt the plan without parental support. Therefore, he arranged with the principal for me to appear on the PTO agenda to discuss Dual Credit. I spoke to the Parent Teacher Organization (PTO) about the Dual Credit Plan and the pros and cons of it for their children. Approximately three hundred parents were present at the meeting that evening. After the presentation, I was asked several questions, which I answered. After limited discussion, the PTO President looked at the principal and said, "we want this plan implemented for our children this fall." I was surprised and also impressed at the ease with which the proposal was embraced and approved. The principal's job at that point, if she wanted to keep her job, was to follow the school district's protocol to make the implementation of dual credit happen. Thus, in fall 1992, dual credit was implemented and is still growing by leaps and bounds even today in that community which is among the most elite in the area with some home values exceeding 1 million dollars and parents who are college educated. This example shows the power, influence, and effect of organized community engagement.

To some degree, it was through the community action that the plan was approved and implemented. If we had limited our discussions to the school administration, it is likely that the red tape of bureaucracy would have slowed the process. Even though dual credit was a significant addition to the educational process at that time and expanded quite rapidly in suburban communities, there were, nonetheless, foot-dragging responses in urban communities to make the program available to low-income students, many of whom were African American and Hispanic. The typical response was, "Well, you know those students do not qualify."

First and foremost, there is a need for a community call to action. Every community in America needs to rally around quality education for the children. There have been books, articles, and reports written about crises in the schools. There have been reports about the high dropout rates as well as the numbers of low-performing schools in various communities. There have been reports of low college readiness among children of color who graduate from the nation's public schools. The information is available, but people look hopelessly at the reports, not knowing what their role can and should be to address the problem. Additionally, there is the assumption that perhaps the problem is with the children, particularly the children of color, that somehow their capacity to learn is limited, their willingness to learn is low, and their cultural experiences somehow restrict their ability to grasp information and apply it constructively. All are false assumptions that blame the victim and allow a system that is not serving all of the children well to continue to relegate some children to low-performing schools. In the end analysis, everyone suffers from that type of thinking—not only the children but the society at large. Thus, a revolution is needed that begins at the grassroots level to promote change in the educational system and to hold schools accountable to ensure that every child is taught by the best-trained teachers with the best curriculum and tools and that students be required to learn maximally. If highly trained educators who are paid high salaries cannot motivate children to learn and cannot impart the knowledge and skills required for students to be competitive, then those educators should have intensive professional development in the proper disciplines to acquire the knowledge and skills needed. If improvement is not demonstrated after proper training, the teachers should be dismissed from the classrooms and reassigned to their areas of strength. If the schools persist and retain those teachers in the classroom without the proper support and development, the message being sent to the public is clear. The message is that the schools lack proper leadership to ensure the educational preparedness of young people.

A student's ability to pass standardized tests has been one measure used to evaluate students' progress and to assess teachers' performance. Standardized tests have been accorded too much weighted value in evaluating students' ability to succeed in school or in life. In fact, standardized tests have been the precise tools used to limit access of many African American students to certain in-demand careers and professions. There should be increased focus on the core competencies that students must learn to pass required courses in mathematics, science, English, government, and other key subjects. And, of course, there is a need for valid and reliable tests that assess the attainment of those competencies. Too many students are failing in the subjects of mathematics and science, reading, writing, and comprehension. So, what is happening during the course of the school day between the time of arrival at school to the time of departure from school to justify the community's support of education when so many students are either failing or dropping out? The answer is clear. Too many students are being taught by instructors who are simply babysitting.

In every profession and every category of employment, the risks to society will become magnified if the community ignores its greater responsibility to the development of an educated society. Think for a moment about the ramifications for a society where there are limited numbers of competent physicians, nurses, lawyers, educators, production workers, technicians, and business people. No one wants to be attended to by health care professionals who barely completed their training with only 75 percent competency when 100 percent competency is the goal. So, when well-meaning people contemplate what every child's education means to their health, welfare, and security, the desire to ensure that every child—no matter the color of skin or ethnic origin—gets a quality education takes on quite a different level of significance and urgency.

Grassroots initiatives among people who have the time and the will must begin to motivate the masses to action to demand more accountability for improved performance in the schools. It is time for the community of supporters of an educated citizenry to ask questions that result in answers why trained educators are not producing greater outcome results among students that they teach every day. It is recommended that the community examine the schools with a critical eye to assess what is occurring to interfere with teaching and learning in each school. If qualified teachers are allowed to teach, then it is my belief that students—no matter the description or level of preparedness—will learn. It is difficult for teachers to become effective transformative educators if they are also managing other major tasks outside of their scope of work. Teachers have their roles to fulfill in service to students. Administrators have their roles to fulfill and so do board members. The community's work is the feet to the fire, probing hard work to ensure that accountability becomes a reality and that student success becomes the norm. Educational engagement by the community is a top priority. The community needs to know the school's vision, mission, and purpose. What is the role of the school? What are the issues at the school, and how the community can help to address the issues? What is the overall and differentiated performance of students in the schools based upon demographics? What is the report card on teachers and their credentials? What is the report card on technology in the schools? What is the report card on the curricula and how students are being prepared to function in a global society? And, what is the school's educational strategic plan?

Typically, some of the most powerful and influential organizations within African American communities address concerns that focus on public education. Unlike the civic associations that address issues pertaining to infrastructure within their communities, crime, low-rent housing, and other social and political concerns, the results that demonstrate improvement in public education are more complex and usually require more time. Usually, the social issues are addressed with great results from elected officials due to their desire for re-election in the next two to four years, their unwavering commitment to the community, and their desire to do the right thing. Within public education, there are no term limits; instead, there are contracts with huge buyout agreements that taxpayers fund if head school administrators do not meet specific goals; in the end analysis, when the well-paid administrators leave their posts, the students are still the victims, left behind to be subjected to failing schools and an uncertain future.

What Is Required for Success

First and foremost, all stakeholders must recognize the urgency of their support to change the downward spiral educationally in their communities and commit to collective action to change the trend. It is essential that they begin to ask questions about student success and teacher preparedness; they should also demand explanations about the low student performance outcomes and the high student dropout rates. Any answers that blame students should be dismissed. It is true that many African American children grow up in single-parent homes. Nevertheless, there are extended family members who help nurture, support, and encourage the children. In many families, young children are raised by grandparents who struggled through years of raising their own children. Despite the structure of the home, the school is where students spend a significant part of their day and where the greatest impact can and should be made to inspire students to learn. The community can make an impact by serving as mentors for students or advisors to the schools.

The statement is true that circumstances can change, for it is people who change their circumstances. That, in my estimation, is what the community engagement can help to achieve. The community must have the will to examine what is happening to African American children and rally around a mandate to ensure quality education for the children. Finally, when the shift occurs and the positive results are realized, it will be clear that proactive and constructive involvement from the community mattered.

Sensitivity to Sociocultural Factors Matters

Sociocultural values and practices can have a major influence in teaching and learning situations. Therefore, a recognition of the social and cultural factors is essential, and sensitivity to them is important in the teaching and learning environment, both for teachers and for students.

When practitioners say, "We have always done this (whatever it is) this way," that statement reflects the kind of attitude that can develop when practices are allowed to become entrenched without periodic review of them, or various traditions are allowed to continue in the schools without regard to the effects on the student populations being served. Professional development is vital to organizations that wish to generate maximum employee performance and maximum student outcomes. One area for professional development that requires an annual tune-up is a review of teachers' emotional readiness to teach at-risk and ethnic-minority student populations. Teachers' emotional health and sociocultural influences can become a major impediment to effective instruction. The second area of focus should regularly address best practices that can be implemented to enhance teaching effectiveness and student learning outcomes. This area is of special importance for African American male students and their success, particularly given the unique set of problems associated with their persistency, performance, and matriculation in school.

Typically, at the beginning of each academic school year, teachers are issued their room assignments, their classroom door keys, the curriculum, and textbooks. There is arguably also a need for a professional development check-in before classes begin to ensure that teachers are intellectually and psychologically ready to undertake a new school year of opportunities and challenges in educating students who reside in urban communities. On numerous occasions, I have heard teachers bemoan the beginning of the academic year. Some talk about the bad kids and the difficult parents. Seldom do I hear comments about the good kids and the supportive parents. It seems that the return to school after a summer vacation stirs the rawest emotions of some teachers—or at least of those who were involved in the conversation that I recently overheard. As I sat and listened, I wondered how the joy of teaching could be restored for those well-meaning, well-qualified practitioners who seemed to be so utterly defeated by the demands of their profession. I have concluded that practitioners need the emotional, psychological, and pedagogical support to maintain their high performance levels. Practitioners bring their sociocultural backgrounds into the classrooms, and students bring theirs, too. They bring their history of past bad educational experiences into the classroom, and the students bring theirs, too. Many teachers do not want to be in the classroom; and not surprisingly, many students do not want to be there either.

So, the attitudes of both teachers and students are important and can complicate the teaching/learning environment even before the first class begins. Those attitudes have the potential to set the tone for the entire school year. Therefore, a focus on the sociocultural factors that can influence both teachers and students are worthy of review. This chapter will present a cursory view of sociocultural factors in an effort to alert educators to their need to be cognizant of this topic's importance and the dynamics associated with the factors that could influence teaching and learning.

WHAT ARE SOCIOCULTURAL FACTORS?

Sociocultural refers to a combination of the social and cultural factors that influence behavior. The social factors include those norms in society that influence how people think and behave. The cultural factors, on the other hand, comprise the mores of sub groups in society that influence the behaviors, practices, attitudes, and beliefs. When the social and the cultural factors are combined, they can have a significant impact on how teachers teach and how students learn. For example, there are some students who work best in collaborative teams, and there are others who work best individually.

In the American culture, for example, eye contact is important; there are other cultural and subcultural groups, however, where eye contact of a subordinate with a person in authority is a sign of disrespect. The work ethic also varies across cultures and across generational classifications wherein some groups feel that a person should work only when it is necessary versus others who believe that work is a common expectation. The sociocultural factors shape how individuals perceive the world and respond to the world around them. These factors also help students shape their view of themselves in the world. Therefore, to avoid the common pitfalls that violate cultural norms and that lead to communication breakdown, it is important for practitioners to understand the general cultural practices and beliefs of the individuals being taught.

Sociocultural factors play a role in educators' ability to effectively connect with African American children to successfully educate them. Those factors also represent one of the major areas for communication breakdown. A failure to understand the nonverbal signs and symbols of groups poses a significant barrier. If the teacher is ethnocentric, the students easily recognize the attitude and resist. The resistance might come in various forms: inattentiveness, missing class, or even dropping out.

Having worked with teachers to observe and critique their teaching effectiveness, it is apparent to me that teachers of all ethnicities and all experiential levels welcome any assistance offered to improve upon their delivery of instruction. Many teachers readily acknowledge, however, that their lessons are prepared for the general population of students instead of being individualized. They cite the lack of time needed to develop their lesson plans as a factor in the disconnect between the subject matter they are teaching and the subject's relevancy to students' lives. Many also express their lack of sufficient knowledge about the African American culture that would allow them to work with students more effectively.

A cultural idiosyncrancy is also prevalent within the African American community about the use of the term *African American* in reference to them. Some say they are not from Africa; they are Americans, born and bred. While *African American* is the nomenclature used to refer to a race of people, the conundrum is that some African Americans differ widely in their view of themselves based upon their educational and economic accomplishments and their economic and social-class status. The interesting distinction is the perspective. Some African Americans view themselves differently and have created levels of economic and class differentiations within the race. Yet, from the

MARGARET FORD FISHER

perspective of those persons outside the race, all African Americans are still essentially the same. They are all considered to be a homogeneous group; and all are treated similarly, irrespective of what some might call the artificial categories within the race that classify individuals based upon economics, education, religion, or social-class status.

The reality for those who have isolated themselves from others in the race and for those who have created incredibly ingenious ways to separate themselves categorically from other African Americans is a shocking, insulting wake-up call to be told, "Yes, you might have accomplished all of these great feats, and you might have set yourself apart from others of your race, but the reality is that all of you are still the same." That sweeping generalization is enough to offend some African Americans who have worked hard to differentiate themselves from the lesser fortunate of the race educationally and economically.

So, as I reflect upon African American children in the schools, they assemble with diverse sociocultural beliefs and perceptions not just of the world around them but from within the race that is used to define them. There are the gradations based upon complexion, hair texture, family background, religion, social club, and the list continues *ad infinitum*. If the teacher is not aware of the intra-cultural values and distinctions and errs by making an inappropriate reference that offends, that factor alone could create dissonance between the student and the teacher. Thus, sensitivity to sociocultural factors matters.

A Focus on the Educational Practitioner

All persons are the product of their history, beliefs, and experiences. For the purposes of illustration, I will group the triad (history, beliefs, experiences) and refer to them as cumulative acquisitions. In this section, cumulative acquisitions is being used not as a negative reference but descriptively and figuratively to illustrate all of everything learned in life that, unless unpacked or eliminated, will always be an influencing factor on an individual's attitudes and behaviors. In this instance, cumulative acquisitions means being loaded with all of the beliefs, stereotypes, myths, past experiences, and prejudices that cause some individuals to have preconceived ideas and closed minds. If an incident occurs that confirms the teacher's belief about a child, the teacher might say, "I knew that was true, and that reaffirms my belief." When something positive happens, the teacher might say, "I'm surprised. I didn't know he had it in him." Beliefs as well as other assumptions that people have are difficult to change. Thus, acquisitions that people carry can appear as perceptual acquisitions that involve what a person senses. Gender acquisitions can appear as differential treatment of individuals based upon whether they are male or female. Psychological acquisitions that involve the mind and emotions can appear as flashbacks to past experiences; and finally, cultural acquisitions involve all of the values, beliefs, and attitudes that are transmitted from one generation to the next. It is important for educators to take stock of themselves and their readiness to teach in an effort to be at their very best to facilitate the intellectual growth and development of students.

TAKING STOCK

The question is, How do you take a negative belief and neutralize it? You accomplish that goal by infusing new information and new experiences to replace the negative beliefs. This is what practitioners are charged to do as they educate students and provide new vistas in students' thinking that can transform their lives. As with anything, work is required to get the desired end product. I remember the impression made upon me years ago that illustrates this point. The story pertains to my grandfather who was a master farmer. One day, I rode with him on his wagon to the family's farm. As we rode along and talked, I asked Grandpa, "Why do the workers have to pick the cotton?" In its raw form, it did not appear very useful. My grandpa responded that making that cotton into something useful was a process that would be completed in stages. Everybody along the way had their jobs to do. "If everyone along the way does their job well," he said, "the cotton will eventually end up as nice garments, beautiful tablecloths, or some other fine product."

The same is true of our educational system and African American students who matriculate and go through the process of educational transformation. If everyone in the process does his job well, then the students will be our highly trained and well-qualified professionals of tomorrow. But everyone at each stage of the process must commit to doing his job well. So, teachers should periodically examine their cumulative acquisitions to determine what is dated, what is unnecessary, and what is inappropriate that they can discard. Then they can consider what new acquisitions are required to rise to their highest peak of performance as educators. It is appropriate that practitioners make a commitment to replace the negative attitudes, experiences, and beliefs with positive ones. This will be a gradual process, but keep in mind that transformation is steady and consistent, and everyone along the way has a job to do. If everyone along the way does his job well, transformative teachers will help usher in the next generation of great educators, scientists, doctors, lawyers, and many other professionals that society needs.

BARRIERS TO TEACHING

Many barriers exist that could potentially interfere with teachers' ability to teach and students' receptivity to learn. The major barriers are grouped into three categories. They are the individual barriers under which sociocultural factors appear, the institutional barriers, and the societal barriers. The barriers are briefly described below.

The individual barriers are those that pertain specifically to the practitioner and that only the practitioner has the ability to change. They comprise the practitioner's cumulative history and provide the filters through which most of their decisions are made. Below is an abbreviated list of individual barriers.

- False Assumptions: False assumptions are not true and are based upon circumstances that are taken for granted.

- Prejudices: Prejudices are attitudes that are formed without a rational basis. Prejudices are also preconceived opinions that are formed without the benefit of reason, knowledge, or thought.

- Stereotypes: Stereotypes are generalizations to describe or characterize a group of people.

- Perceptions: Perceptions are the conclusions drawn as a result of using the senses to acquire information about people or situations.

- Beliefs: Beliefs are mental states where individuals hold propositions or premises to be true.

- Personal History: Personal history is the cumulative background of a person that he can remember that impacts thinking and relationships with others.

- Culture: Culture is the combination of values, beliefs, and practices of a group that are transmitted from one generation to the next.

- Ethnicity: Ethnicity refers to a group of individuals who share a common heritage, ancestry, language, and distinctiveness.

- Worldview: Worldview is a mindset that reflects how individuals see the world around them, how they relate to people, to society, and to existence.

The above list is not exhaustive, but it provides some of the most common areas that could be a source of concern and result in discrimination against African American children. No doubt, children develop similar barriers that influence their thinking and their behaviors. Teachers as authority figures have the ability to play the leading role to remove the barriers that separate teachers and students as human beings who, as humans, aspire for the same ideals: life, liberty, and the pursuit of happiness.

The second category includes institutional barriers. The institutional barriers are outside of the teacher's ultimate sphere of control but can have a negative impact upon the teacher, the teacher's morale, and the teacher's delivery of quality instruction. Institutional barriers do not develop in isolation. Institutions are operated by people who bring their diverse histories, values, beliefs, and practices to the institution to either govern, fund, or administer the operations. Changing institutions is more difficult than changing individuals. With the individual, only one person is involved. To change institutions requires changing many individuals and their collective thoughts. This process applies to any institution: public schools, colleges, universities, and all others. Results of institutional barriers include inadequate funding to serve students, inadequate facilities, obsolete technology, limited qualified faculty, limited staff, low standards and low expectations for African American students.

The final category is comprised of the societal barriers. The societal barriers are the ones that practitioners have even less control over. The societal barriers are reflective of the broader history of the predominant group in society and of the wishes of the group in power. When the stability of society is threatened, those in power have the authority and the ability to make systemic changes. Societal barriers include the laws that are made by which individuals rule and govern. The Jim Crow laws during the era of slavery were a societal barrier that limited opportunities for individuals based upon race. Societal barriers can be rectified by the collective will of the people. That right is reflective of the democratic process by which laws are made and laws are changed.

CONCLUSION

So, the job of a teacher is not an easy one. Teachers have a significant number of challenges to respond to that could easily distract them from their primary role, which is teaching. In addition to the many barriers and challenges, they also have to inspire children to learn. These are formidable challenges that this book will help the practitioners to address. The educational system has not, in all instances, devoted sufficient time to equipping practitioners with the moral support and the required tools to do their jobs well. The process has, in some instances, resembled a charade, particularly in those schools that have consistently hired out-of-field teachers to teach core subjects to African American children. Having been a public school teacher in the early stages of my career and having worked with teachers in their professional development, it is clear that too many of the wrong demands are placed upon teachers that distract them from their primary role and function. What do you think would happen if teachers could devote their time exclusively to teaching and creating the proper conditions to empower all of their students to learn? The results could be profound. Profound results are what society needs. Meanwhile, sociocultural factors cannot and should not be ignored. They are often the driving forces behind what takes place in the classroom, "good, bad, or indifferent."

Student Ethos and Resiliency Matter

If you want to see the representation of ethos and resiliency, look at the people who have endured hardships and challenges yet have overcome them. They have bounced back from their adversity and are now more convicted and more determined than ever. In the context of this book concentrating on African American children and preparing them for success, I encourage the readers to focus on successful individuals who have overcome great challenges to ultimately accomplish their goals in life. For a more personal example of those who persisted, you can see them in your everyday encounters among colleagues and friends who will tell how they overcame their challenges to be where they are today. Of course, you, the reader, have your story of survival as well. For those who did not persist, you can see them every day, pushing their grocery carts down the street with all of their worldly possessions contained therein or living under the viaducts in any urban city of the country. Others are incarcerated because the only way they knew to cope was through social deviance; and finally, others are deceased and are unable to tell their stories or to offer advice about how to stay focused in the midst of challenges.

Everyone, no matter the age or the ethnicity, has challenges. Some challenges are absolutely daunting. However, to avoid many of the challenges that people face in life requires common sense and good judgment. This chapter focuses on ethos and resiliency and how practitioners can assist African American students to develop both.

What Is Ethos and Why Is It Important?

Ethos refers to the driving force or set of beliefs that compel and motivate individuals. Each person has a desire for achievement in life; but for various reasons, many fall short of accomplishing their goals. While the ethos is essential, there are other influencing factors that help undergird and sustain a person's quest for success. The following themes represent comments from focus groups of students in minority studies classes that reflect what sustained them and what they think can sustain others in their drive to achieve success in life. This information, I think, is pertinent to the success of African American children and is synopsized below.

Encouragement from Significant People in Their Lives

The two operative words are *encouragement* and *significant*. Encouragement from significant people who have distinguished themselves in a particular field, people whose opinions that you value, and people that you care about is obviously very important. No doubt, the encouragement bolsters the personal confidence and self-esteem. Couple the encouragement with support from parents who ensure that their children have all of the educational and social development experiences needed and then who position their children to excel in all that they do. This is the experience of some individuals, and they are fearless in their approach to life and to life's challenges. They believe that they can succeed, and they do. The encouragement they receive further solidifies their drive to accomplish their goals.

A Competitive Spirit

The conditioning that children learn in their everyday lives is to be competitive. Despite the impoverished conditions that some children live in, many of them still have the drive and the determination to compete – and yes to win. Despite the defeats, many of them still hone their talents and skills to compete again and to ultimately be victorious. This is the attitude and spirit that has catapulted many individuals to success. In focus group meetings, students indicated that their involvement in competitive events equipped them with the mindset to win and the advice to get up and try again if there was a loss. This competitive spirit is thought to be an essential component that allows a person to rise above mediocrity. They are the ones who believe the wise admonition that says, "If you try and don't succeed, try, try again." That exhilaration that comes from winning and being the best has permeated many levels of society. However, some children have lost the competitive zeal in their personal lives. Learning for Ownership can help rekindle the desire among children to set realistic goals and to begin to win.

Personal Beliefs

People have to believe in themselves. Belief in self is a requirement for success. If you tell some individuals they cannot succeed, that becomes their drive to prove that they can. They believe that they are over comers, and they demonstrate that through their actions. Focus group members spoke about the limitations that others tried to impose upon them. Others' biases against them propelled them to success. The negative statements presented the challenge that encouraged them to enroll in college or to seek a better life. These examples are not to suggest that negative feedback or criticism of others is preferred. It simply suggests that the self-fulfilling prophecies do not always have the intended effect.

A Positive Influence of Role Models

Sometimes, individuals need to see examples of success through role models who look like them or who come from similar backgrounds to comprehend that success for them is also possible. That is an influencing factor that sometimes motivates them to strive for a better life. In the Deep South prior to the Civil Rights movement, the majority of black professionals were preachers and teachers. Their status influenced other blacks to follow in their footsteps at that time and even today. As access to more career fields and opportunities have broadened for African Americans, there are more blacks who are convinced that they can pursue those career pathways as well.

A Record of Cumulative Success

Individuals are validated when they achieve success. When the success accumulates, the self-confidence and the self-esteem also increase. There are some individuals who have been successful in every venture and have achieved every goal. They only know what it is like to be successful. Their confidence is bold. Even from their youth, they developed a history of success and became true believers that people create their successes and failures, first in their minds.

A Hunger and Passion for a Better Life

A hunger and passion for a better life is the mindset that propels some to great heights in life. They look at their current circumstances and the lives of those around them and decide they want more for themselves. The critical factor is for them to know what the options are that lie before them and how to prepare to pursue their dreams. Unfortunately, many African American students do not know their options, so they choose from the limited menu of what they see glamorized. It is important for young people to dream early in life to imagine what they can become, for there is more to life than what they can physically see in their neighborhoods or in the sitcoms on television. Educational practitioners can help the students broaden their vision. It is necessary to stretch the possibilities so children can learn about the multiple ways they can realize and fulfill their potential and have a productive life.

A Champion for a Cause to Benefit Humanity

I am amazed by the number of successes that people achieve because early in life they knew a beloved relative who had a health challenge or who experienced an alleged injustice, so they wanted to become a physician or a scientist to find a cure to the specific problem, or they wanted to pursue a legal career to make right a perceived wrong and to prevent a future miscarriage of justice. Benefitting humanity was a recurring theme among participants that connected them to their drive to succeed.

Success Is the Only Option

Finally, some individuals know that for them, success is the only option. They know the circumstances of their current life and choose not to live the rest of their lives under depressed and oppressive conditions. They view anything less than success, including mediocrity, as failure. They know that they want a better life and make the sacrifices necessary to achieve their goal.

The driving force or ethos, as mentioned earlier, is essential. If the drive is strong enough, that drive will help individuals persist through adversity to accomplish their goals. What is absolutely necessary in all of the categories, however, is the ability to think critically, to exercise good judgment, and to make the correct moral and ethical choices.

THE ETHOS DIRECTIONAL SCALE

In the illustration that follows, the Ethos Directional Scale, there are two opposite poles. One is positive, and the other is negative. Consider the cumulative effect of positive ethos-generating factors versus the cumulative effect of the negative. Without doubt, the experiences, whether positive or negative influence the students' stamina and drive for success. It is those differences that institutions often have to discover and grapple with to ensure students' persistency in school.

So, how strong is the student's personal drive and will to succeed? That question is answered partially in the Ethos Directional Scale. The scale is a first-step attempt to begin a conversation with children about resiliency and ethos. The scale incorporates three themes from Aristotle's view of the chief components of ethos. Those components are goodwill, practical wisdom, and virtue – all of which practitioners desire that their students develop and practice. (Kraut, Richard, "Aristotle's Ethics," the Stanford Encyclopedia of Philosophy, Summer 2010 Edition, Edward N. Zalta (ed.) URL=http://plato, Stanford, edu/archives/Sum 2010/entries/Aristotle–ethics/)

ETHOS DIRECTIONAL SCALE

Survey

Instructions: Circle one response to each statement that reflects your answer. The scoring values and the meaning of each follow: *On the negative side, the values indicate the following: -3 = "At*

No Time - Never" : -2 ="Not Under Any Condition": -1 = "Not in Any Way"

Zero is the midpoint that separates the two sides of the scale. On the positive side, +1 = "Sometimes"; + 2 = "Frequently," +3 = "Always"

Indicate Your Answer to Each Statement Below:

<u>Student Perspective</u>

I have a strong will.

    -3   -2   -1   0   +1   +2   +3

When challenging situations arise, I work to overcome the challenges.

    -3   -2   -1   0   +1   +2   +3

I rely on my intuitive abilities before making a decision.

    -3   -2   -1   0   +1   +2   +3

I am an over comer.

    -3   -2   -1   0   +1   +2   +3

I believe I can achieve.

    -3   -2   -1   0   +1   +2   +3

I live by principles.

    -3   -2   -1   0   +1   +2   +3

When people try to keep me down, I come back stronger.

    -3   -2   -1   0   +1   +2   +3

I am driven to achieve my goals.

    -3   -2   -1   0   +1   +2   +3

I am determined to fulfill my dreams.

    -3   -2   -1   0   +1   +2   +3

I will do anything to succeed.

-3   -2   -1   o   +1   +2   +3

I know exactly what I want to become in life.

-3   -2   -1   o   +1   +2   +3

I believe in success, and I try to help my friends believe in success, too.

-3   -2   -1   o   +1   +2   +3

I am patient with others.

-3   -2   -1   o   +1   +2   +3

I will go out of my way to help another person.

-3   -2   -1   o   +1   +2   +3

I give up easily.

-3   -2   -1   o   +1   +2   +3

I am a virtuous person.

-3   -2   -1   o   +1   +2   +3

I believe in goodwill toward others.

-3   -2   -1   o   +1   +2   +3

I make wise choices.

-3   -2   -1   o   +1   +2   +3

I am self-reliant.

-3   -2   -1   o   +1   +2   +3

I exercise good judgment.

-3   -2   -1   o   +1   +2   +3

I am a critical thinker.

-3   -2   -1   o   +1   +2   +3

I rely heavily on others to decide for me.

⁻3	⁻2	⁻1	0	+1	+2	+3

I believe in the just treatment of all persons.

⁻3	⁻2	⁻1	0	+1	+2	+3

I practice good, moral behavior.

⁻3	⁻2	⁻1	0	+1	+2	+3

In the Ethos Directional Scale, the student has the opportunity to respond to the items and engage in one-on-one conversations with the teacher about the responses and how the tool can be an insightful and helpful self-development project for them. The task for practitioners is to take the results and, as will be discussed in the chapter on Learning for Ownership, help position the student for success.

To use the scale in working with students, it is recommended that teachers ask the students to be honest in their responses, for there are no right or wrong answers. Then it is recommended that the teacher explain the values on the scale. After the survey has been completed, the instructor can tabulate the responses, showing the tendencies of students as they examine the strength of their ethos. This survey can help highlight the interventions that teachers can make.

On the negative side of the scale, the negative values are represented with the negative (-) sign. On the positive side of the scale, the values are represented with the positive (+) sign. The scale and its numbers represent the following. Zero is neutral and indicates that the student does not have a positive or negative response. The negative 1 indicates "Not in Any Way," the negative 2 indicates "Not under Any Condition," and the negative 3 indicates "At No Time, Never." The range of scores is provided to assess the intensity of students' responses. On the positive side of the scale, the positive 1 indicates "Sometimes," the positive 2 indicates "Frequently," and the positive 3 indicates "Always."

The Importance of Resiliency

Resiliency describes an individual's ability to recover from hardship, negative pressure, temporary defeats, loss, and criticism while incrementally growing in resolve. Resiliency is the fiber and sinew developed as a result of adversity. The resiliency draws upon the mental toughness, the mental training, and the belief system that allows individuals to keep everything in perspective and not be permanently overpowered by the circumstances of life. Some people are easily discouraged by criticism from others. One defeat is more than enough for some; for others, one loss is too great to bear. Yet, to increase a child's fiber and sinew of resiliency, the child must know the ways to maintain focus and stability during adverse situations. Why is it that some people have greater resiliency than others? Even within the same families, irrespective of social or economic class, siblings will display differing levels of resiliency. In part, their differences in responses are based upon experiences and beliefs.

Resiliency develops and grows under adverse circumstances. The role of institutions is to assist the students to accomplish their educational goals while helping to fortify their response mechanisms to the adverse pressures that could deter them from persisting toward their educational goals. Institutions should provide students with the opportunity to brainstorm responses to real-life scenarios and discover solutions to potential problems they may encounter. A network of support should be developed through peer groups and mentors that will provide the guidance that is required. Additionally, for many, the support of their churches, their families, extended families, and friends can help create the base necessary to sustain them to achieve success.

ETHOS AND RESILIENCY MATTER

To have a driving force without the commitment and the determination to sustain it is akin to having a high-powered vehicle without the gasoline to drive it. Educators should view all children as capable. They have the essential parts necessary to accomplish great things. The question is simple. What are the people most responsible for the children teaching them? Are they being fueled with the right information and the right perspectives to propel them toward the achievement of their lifetime goals?

Communication Matters

For nine years, I taught minority studies courses at a Midwestern University. Prior to that time, I had the pleasure of teaching English and African American Studies courses at the local high school in the same city. The minority studies program was relatively new, and my focus as assistant professor was to teach courses about the history of African Americans, Mexican Americans, and Native American Indians in the United States. As a part of the curriculum, I taught interpersonal and cross-cultural communications courses, highlighting among other topics the polarization and strife that can occur as a result of differing values, differing political interests, and differing communication styles. The differing communication styles were intriguing and included the assertive, aggressive, passive, or passive-aggressive styles, each with its potential impact on communication. The assertive style of communication is the most preferred but the least used. This style involves negotiation and a win-win solution. The aggressive style of communication is the forceful style of communication that involves manipulation and control. The passive communication style is the type that seeks to avoid confrontation. The passive-aggressive style avoids direct confrontation but is manipulative and cunning. With the study of interpersonal communication, it was fascinating to observe how the shared values of individuals brought them closer together. The lessons were always pertinent, and I think I enjoyed preparing for my classes just as much as my students enjoyed listening to the lectures and participating in the class discussions. Finally, in my doctoral program, I completed a degree in curriculum and instruction with an emphasis on English and multicultural studies. Throughout my teaching experiences and my studies domestically and abroad, I have always been intrigued by the complexity of communication and the various points at which a breakdown in communication can occur and lead to misunderstandings and conflicts, even to wars. This is a problem that can sometimes be avoided; nevertheless, the signs and symbols of language and dialects create a potential cauldron of conflicting interpretations, even with the most seasoned communicators, that make effective communication a challenge at best. The challenge to communicate effectively is not isolated to crosscultural groups, nor is it guaranteed that communication will be effective when conducted among groups with the same shared dialects and the same shared history.

Effective communication is important, however, from the preparation and dissemination of information to the verbal and nonverbal interactions with others. While communication may create dissension if the message is negative, absolute failure to communicate is problematic as well and can result in irreparable damage to relationships. Communication is the process of sending information from one person to another. According to the Sapir-Whorf hypothesis, communication is a product of our language. Thus, the language and thought are intertwined and affect the way people think and behave. In the context of this work, communication is addressed from a broad perspective as it affects schools. The focus narrows to address African American youth, the dialects that are spoken, the nonverbal communication that is transmitted, and the necessity for students to improve their communication skills to achieve a measure of success in society. The statement made by Dr. Asa Hilliard resonates once again in this chapter to further illustrate the power and effect of both the verbal and nonverbal communication. He indicated that teachers are always teaching, good, bad, or indifferent, and students are always learning, good, bad, or indifferent.

AVOIDING COMMON PITFALLS TO EFFECTIVE COMMUNICATION

In any relationship with another person or with a group, there are some common expectations. One of the most common is that individuals in the relationship will receive information about matters that affect them. This is true no matter if the relationship is superordinate/subordinate or a relationship of peers. When that expectation is unmet, there is the perception of disrespect and the feeling of insignificance. Common pitfalls that should be avoided include the following: the failure to communicate, the use of inappropriate use of verbal and nonverbal signs and symbols, and a deviation from the standard dialect in an attempt to curry favor and communicate with diverse audiences. Examples are provided to illustrate the problems that can occur in each instance.

In my first high school teaching assignment, I became aware of the complexities of communication and the passive style of relating to others that led to turmoil and strife. My first teaching assignment was in what had been a segregated part of the city where mostly lower-income residents lived. It was an area where the confederate flag still waved proudly in the community as well as on the flag pole in front of the school building. People were still feeling the residual effects of the Civil Rights movement and the passage of major laws guaranteeing civil rights and voting rights to African Americans. With the availability of radio and television news as well as front-page newspaper articles about racial conflicts in various parts of the country, everyone was aware of the incendiary nature of desegregation for so many individuals. While there had not been any major disturbances in the town where I lived during the entirety of the Civil Rights movement, that distinction was about to change. Without any preparation or announcements to the general school community, buses loaded with African American children from the inner-city communities began to arrive at the school, and the newcomers to the high school began to unload and enter the school building. Apparently, except for the central administration, the principal, and maybe a few others, no one else I talked to knew about all of the new students who would be enrolling at the school. The setting became tense almost immediately and remained that way for the duration of the school year. Every other week thereafter, there were student disruptions and/or all-out riots in the hallways, in the classrooms, and in the parking lot of the campus.

As a new instructor, I was only one of two African Americans on the instructional staff. As far as I know, my arrival had not been announced either. My schedule included teaching three hours of English courses to what became a racially diverse student population and two hours of African American history to predominantly black students. That combination created an interesting shift of gears during the day and an interesting dynamic. There were some occasions when I could not begin the lessons immediately because the tension in the air was too thick; tempers were flaring because someone had been called a disparaging name,and students were beginning to choose sides. Students were on edge and simply not ready to listen to a lecture, so I usually took a few minutes to allow students to express their feelings and to channel their energy into a positive direction before proceeding with the lesson for the day.

The dynamics created a case study example of a pitfall to be avoided. That pitfall is a failure to communicate. The poor, innocent victims were the students. Students were reacting to situations, despite not having all the facts, as though they were reliving the Civil War. How ironic I thought to see the students' reactions when they saw busloads of African American children unloading at the front door of the school and entering the building. These were children who, under other circumstances, could be friends; but a combination of mishaps, miscues, and missed opportunities to communicate created an environment where students became adversaries instead. Students reacted as though they were protecting their turf from invasion by the unwelcome intruders, and many of them were willing to fight to defend it. The African American students, on the other hand, were viewed as part of an incursion that they did not fully understand, yet they were the trailblazers who, nonetheless, walked into a setting almost like a war zone in an effort to make a positive difference. That experience was a time to be remembered by me and by others for years to come. I often think that this was the point at which communication would have made a difference. That was the time when the leadership of the school could have briefed students before their new schoolmates arrived to update the students on what was mandated and to ask for their support and cooperation as the school embarked upon this new transition. It was a time also for African American students who arrived at the school to know the issues they would potentially confront. Something could have been said; instead, nothing was said. In fact, many of the students claimed they did not know where they were going until they ended up at the school. So, the lack of communication, verbally, by those in authority was still a communication nonverbally to the students and staff at the school. The perceived message was that everyone in the building was inconsequential and insignificant. From that experience, I learned the importance of effective communication not just to convey a message to one person but to share essential information with everyone who will be affected by change and to solicit their support. This is a case where an assertive style of leadership could have resulted in a different outcome. Think about how the bitterness and hard feelings could have been averted by simple communication. The students on both sides responded to the agitation of the other, and the message conveyed to the general community was that the students could not get along. Maybe the message should have been that the administration handled the situation poorly.

The second pitfall to effective communication is the inappropriate use of verbal and nonverbal signs and symbols. Inappropriate use of the terms of endearment that might be used with one group cannot be taken for granted by others and used in referring to persons of that group. Slang expressions as well as the inappropriate use of terms might not be well received and could result in negative responses. This unfortunate situation has happened on many occasions when well-meaning individuals have simply crossed the line from acceptable to unacceptable word choices and expressions. While the receiver of the message was not offended directly, there were those nearby who heard the demeaning or pejorative references and were offended, thereby resulting in severe consequences.

The third pitfall is a deviation from the standard dialect in formal communication. This problem arises when a speaker tries to appear cool or appeal to a particular group. The risk that the speaker runs is greater than the benefit that will be achieved. This situation has occurred on countless occasions as well. One incident that happened was with a well-respected older Caucasian gentleman who was speaking to a diverse audience of African Americans. In an attempt to break the ice and add humor to his speech or perhaps connect with his audience, he said, "You and I have something in common. I'm a brotha too." No one laughed. In fact, they looked at each other curiously, not quite knowing how to interpret the statement. Had they just been insulted? Was it a joke? Was it an innocent attempt to connect with his audience? At the end of the speech, the gentleman speaker indicated that he had a younger brother who looked up to him as a role model.

It is clear that communication breakdown can occur at any point between the sender and the receiver. Robert McCloskey, former state department spokesman, illustrated the point quite well when he said, "I know that you believe you understood what you think I said, but I am not sure you realize that what you heard is not what I meant."

How to Communicate with Diverse Groups

In communications, the messages can be easily confused and misinterpreted. First and foremost, it is important for instructors to remember that the standard dialect is always appropriate to use in the classroom. Students should also be expected to use the same. The standard dialect is the preferred and is accepted by society as the dialect to use for success. In all situations, teachers must be cognizant of the lessons they are teaching students both through their verbal and nonverbal instructions and behaviors. Teachers should ask themselves the following question. How should I interact with diverse groups in a way to communicate effectively? Using the standard dialect creates a common platform that prepares students to become more proficient verbally and nonverbally to compete on a global stage. This approach is not recommended to diminish other dialects, such as Ebonics, that hold value, but as long as the competitive platform is proficiency in the standard dialect nationally and internationally, then African American students must be prepared to compete on that platform.

Many teachers today are conflicted about whether to allow Ebonics to be the standard used for African American students in the classroom. My response can be summed up in one question: Will proficiency in Ebonics prepare the high school graduates to gain employment with Fortune 500 companies or even to gain employment with the local school districts in key influential positions?

COMMUNICATING WITH YOUNG PEOPLE

Children are people too and are entitled to respect. I recall being invited to speak to a group of ninth-grade girls at a middle school in a large urban area. There were about three hundred girls in the auditorium for their educational development program. Three speakers preceded me, and all three speakers were booed. This response from the young girls surprised me and also momentarily shook my confidence. I could only think as I sat waiting for my turn to speak that I would be booed also and the word would certainly be communicated to my institution before I could return. Finally, my turn came to speak. I gave my talk for the fifteen minutes allocated to me. At the end, I was not booed; instead, I was applauded by the students. What made the difference? The difference was that I asked for their permission, their attention, and their support. I told them that I was invited there to talk to them about a specific topic. I asked for one of the students to serve as time keeper for me. A student in the audience volunteered. Then I asked if they would listen and not boo me. They all agreed. After they all agreed, I began my talk.

That experience taught me a valuable lesson. Often, young people are not respected as they should be, and adults have the tendency on many occasions to simply force themselves upon children without the children's permission. The children's responses are saying, "We are people too. Respect us," and I agree. This experience quickly reminded me of my high school where the events might not have been as volatile if the students had only been given the opportunity to say to the principal: "Yes, Mr. Principal, we will work with you to make the desegregation of students into our school a smooth transition."

The Role of Practitioners

Students are in the process of development; therefore, educators are charged with the responsibility to ensure that all students learn the skills that will prepare them for life. Effective communication is one of those skills. Students should know the effect of their verbal communication in terms of their speech and tone of voice in communicating with others. They should also understand the impact of their nonverbal communication in terms of body language, eye contact with others, and gestures.

To prepare African American students for success, practitioners should, once again, know that it is appropriate to teach African American youth the standard forms of communication. Standard English is what will help advance their acceptance into polite society and will enhance their career opportunities once they graduate from high school. It is not acceptable to limit them to nonstandard forms of communicating.

Not surprisingly, I have heard numerous examples about high school and college graduates who have been overlooked for jobs due to their poor communication skills. In conversation with a diversity coach at a major firm, she identified some of the serious mistakes that young people, particularly African American job prospects, make in their communication that costs them employment opportunities. Poor grammar, slang expressions, and incorrect word choices were often cited. She said, "They did not know they were speaking Ebonics, and that it is unacceptable in the job market."

In African American communities, students learn from people that they are in contact with on a regular basis. They learn the culture of their environment and abide by the cultural standards of their community. Unfortunately, so many students believe that to speak correctly or to dress according to the norms of the society is a process of selling out or trying to be white. The students must overcome that negative programming because their future and their success will depend upon it. For students to believe they can limit their skills to the nonstandard ones and still achieve traditional successes in life is living in denial. Sigmund Freud used this term to categorize people in his study who were faced with facts that were too uncomfortable to accept, and they rejected the facts instead, insisting that they were not true despite what might be overwhelming evidence.

Helping Students Invest in Themselves

I attended a seminar at a local school where the dean of the business department was talking to high school students about the importance of sales and marketing. One of the key points made to the group was that they, the youth, are their best salespeople. As they grow and develop, they should always keep in mind that they are marketing themselves through their appearance, their speech, and their interactions with others. They are the ones who will create the impressions in the minds of others that they are special or that they are just common and ordinary. So, the question was, "As you, the students, learn to network with others, what kind of impression do you want to create and what thoughts do you want to linger long after the conversation has ended?" That is the question for teachers and for students. How do you package and market yourself to make the right impression? Many African American students are conscientious about their appearance and their dress. The question is, What does the dress communicate about them? Are they sending the proper messages and the proper images? If not, what do they need to change and how? This is where the teacher, role models, and mentors intervene to assist with the total development of the young people.

It is important for teachers to be the role models for the young people they teach. The teacher has always been an inspiration for students and should continue to be the example that illumines the path for students to follow.

Conclusion

As we reflect upon the work of noted philosophers and educators, their view is that education is life and not just a preparation for life. If educators agree with that premise, every effort should be made to ensure that African American children understand the consequences of their choices. This is where communication matters. Students should be able to identify their role models and study their mannerisms, how they talk, how they dress, and how they interact with others.

Have you ever had information that was critical to a person's success but you did not share it? How did you feel knowing that your insights could have changed that person's life? That is what is happening with African American children. Everyone knows that African American children have to speak and dress according to the norms of society in order to be positioned for unlimited success. This does not at all negate their ability to operate in multiple subcultural groups and to speak multiple nonstandard dialects; but the primary, dominant culture has certain expectations. To deny the children exposure to the information they need and the training they must have is a major injustice to those children and the future they could have access to in life.

Part Two

Part two of this work is a corollary to part one. After school districts have addressed the basics of what matters in urban education, they can enhance teachers' toolkit to work with African American students through the use of a Typology for Success Plan and a Learning for Ownership Empowerment Model. Both are presented in the following chapters.

Teaching African American Student Populations

In Ralph Ellison's award-winning novel, *Invisible Man*, he said, "I am invisible understand, simply because people refuse to see me…When they approach me, they see only my surroundings, themselves, or figments of their imagination—indeed, everything and anything except me" (Ellison, 7). This description accurately portrays the way some individuals, irrespective of race or ethnicity, respond to African Americans. They are, to them, invisible. Have you ever experienced a person's glance in your direction with their eyes focusing on everyone and everything nearby but you? It appears, at that moment, that their eyes are trained to deliberately look over you. Or have you noticed the eyes of a person focused directly on you, and when the person gets close enough to you to speak, you acknowledge him but there is no reciprocal response? This, in part, is what Ellison describes as that treatment of invisibility. The argument by some, however, is that the cultural meanings associated with eye contact and the cultural rules associated with acknowledging strangers might be influencing the behavior. These arguments are valid and important to accept. However, when the treatment is consistent from teachers and others that you know, then questions arise about the stereotypes and preconceived attitudes that could be influencing their behavior. No doubt, deeply held beliefs can be so ingrained that stimulus/response types of behaviors are the only result unless a deliberate attempt is made to change the response.

Nevertheless, one wonders how long is a reasonable time frame to have a recurrence of this treatment (whether caused by oversight, stereotypes, or prejudice) before the person becomes bitter? How long after bitterness develops is a reasonable time frame before the person reacts? Children experience the feeling of invisibility in the classroom when the teacher asks a question and the only African American child in the classroom continually raises a hand to answer the question and is never acknowledged. The same is true when the teacher calls the roll but somehow either forgets to call the name of the African American student or fails to pronounce the name correctly. Questions may begin to arise in the child's mind followed by feelings of resentment and anger. When there are eventual outbursts, onlookers may gasp and wonder why. "What could have caused the strange behavior?" they ask. Well, the crisis was mounting all the time with each disrespectful act until one day, the student reached the tipping point. Many students have not learned the coping skills to buffer them from insults. According to research studies, African American children, particularly girls, are vulnerable to the feedback from their teachers, and they try to perform in ways that please them. Does an outward display of disrespect toward them lead to other problems that are evident in schools: high attrition, low performance, low completion? This chapter discusses many of the challenges surrounding the education of African American children and the efficacy of tools to strengthen the children's self-esteem, self-concept, and their desire to persist in school and complete their education.

MARGARET FORD FISHER

A Review of the Literature

Data show what could be looming prospects for society if students enrolled at K-12 schools are not motivated to persist and attain core skills and competencies. US Census Bureau data indicates that 50 percent of the US population will be comprised of African Americans and Hispanics by the year 2050. Additionally, the Alliance for Excellent Education reported that African American children are currently disproportionately concentrated in high-poverty, low-performing schools. The children are vulnerable to poor educational outcomes that undermine their chances for success in life and are notably falling behind their white counterparts in graduation rates, literacy rates, and college preparedness rates. In a report to the US House of Representatives Committee on Education and Labor, witnesses reported that the US high school dropout crisis poses one of the greatest threats to the nation's economic growth and competitiveness. The chair of the committee is quoted as saying, "The crisis we're seeing in our nation's high schools is real, it's urgent, and it must be fixed." The house panel comprised of representatives from John Hopkins University, the McKinsey Corporation, and representatives from charter schools and from industry reported that, "Seven thousand students drop out every day and only about 70 percent of students graduate." The McKinsey Corporation indicated that if minority student performance had reached that of white students' in 1998, the gross domestic product (GDP) in 2009 would have been between $310 billion and $525 billion higher, or approximately 2 to 4 percent of Gross Domestic Product (GDP). The achievement gaps in this country are the same as having a permanent national recession, according to the McKinsey Report. Reports further indicate that the minority populations are becoming the majority in many public schools throughout the nation; therefore, approaches and strategies must be implemented to create a twenty-first century success-oriented culture.

Reducing the dropout rate is only one of the challenges that must be addressed. The second challenge is that of motivating and empowering students to learn. The 21st Century Workforce Commission of the National Alliance of Business indicates the urgency in their report on twenty-first century skills. They said:

> The driving force for the 21st century is the intellectual capital of citizens. Political, social, and economic advances in the United States during the millennium will be possible only if the intellectual potential of America's youth is developed now. When there is a history of low performance and high dropout rates among students in urban schools, a new model must be introduced to ensure that students acquire the skill sets required to compete.

As the National Alliance indicates, "It should be no surprise that *what* students learn—as well as how they learn it and *how often* they must refresh these skills—is changing."

This book presents a model to address the issues of failing schools that are failing African American children. Without doubt, the American Public Education System is caught in a dilemma that, when solved, will provide best practice solutions for the world of K-12 education for all students in general but for African American students in particular. With the masses of students from lower socio-economic groups dominating the enrollments in many urban public schools, the challenge for teachers to retain students, motivate them to learn, and equip them with the essential knowledge and skills necessary to function in a global society is, at first blush, a daunting responsibility. The responsibility is needlessly complex and discourages many of the most promising educators from staying in the profession due to performance measures based upon student aptitude scores and school ratings that might have been compromised by years of educational neglect, politics, social promotions, and inconsistent standards and practices within the educational system. Nevertheless, the problem and its potential consequences are real. The problem within the educational system is multifaceted and escalates in its potential damage and effect when schools are unable to cultivate, first and foremost, the mindsets and skill sets within their students that empower them for success. Data gathered in recent studies continue to show the following: low student performance outcomes among many economically disadvantaged and ethnic minority youth, high student dropout rates, low college-readiness and workforce-readiness rates, and increasingly high juvenile delinquency rates. The problem surrounding students and schools has resulted in debates and town hall meetings exploring interventions about short-term and long-term strategies to fix the problem. The core of the problem is age old: how to develop a pedagogy that will motivate students to learn. The solution does not reside in deep structural changes to the educational system; instead, the solutions reside in the human capital that shares the vision for student success and that is aligned properly to achieve positive outcomes.

African American Children and Learning

Brain-based learning theory contends that everyone can learn as long as the brain is not prohibited from fulfilling its natural processes. It is, as the researchers contend, the traditional schooling that often inhibits children's ability to learn by ignoring, discouraging, or punishing the brain's natural learning processes. Some of the additional reasons that the brain might be impaired are through drug use, injury, birth defects, or disease.

According to the United States Department of Health and Human Services, drugs can alter the important brain areas. The brain stem, for example, controls the critical functions such as heart rate, breathing, and sleeping. The limbic system of the brain controls the reward circuit and is responsible for perception of emotions both positive and negative. The cerebral cortex, which is divided into two parts, controls equally important functions. One part of the cerebral cortex controls the senses that enable individuals to see, hear, feel, taste, and smell. The frontal cortex is the thinking center that powers the ability to think, plan, solve problems, and make decisions.

Additional research conducted on the brain by the 21st Century Learning Initiative provides significant findings that are relevant to creating pedagogy for children. In a recent, long-term study, it was found that "four of the five greatest predictors of eventual success at a college or university are applied and achieved before a child even enters school." Those factors are the quantity and quality of discussion in the child's home, the clarity of value systems, strong peer group support, and the amount of independent reading. Inquisitiveness is said to drive children's learning, and constructivism is the theory that cognitive scientists have devised to explain how a child progresses from inquisitiveness to new knowledge. What do you surmise is the conversation taking place in the homes of many African American children? What are the values you think are being taught in urban communities? Who are the peers that are being nurtured, and who are the people providing support of children? What is the literature that the majority of African American children are reading? If inquisitiveness really does drive student learning, what do you think African American children are inquisitive about? If the majority of African American children are enrolling in school without these basic foundational skills, the research indicates that they are already far behind their counterparts. The involvement of parents and key stakeholders is essential to help the schools supplement instruction when formal school is not in session.

To reiterate the scientific findings, "If the brain is not prohibited from fulfilling its natural processes, everyone can learn." So, if other children can learn, African American children can learn as well, irrespective of the perceived loss of time in their early childhood years. Having reviewed the literature and studied the principles about children and how they learn, my premise is that the primary factors affecting African American children are the subcultural conditioning and the real-life experiences that influence their self-image, their personality, and their personal choices. Real-life issues include poverty, unemployment of one or both parents, discrimination, the role of the family in the child's life, child abuse, and drug abuse. These are the areas that complicate children's lives and require attention if children are to make great strides in their learning.

Improving the Human Capital

As you know, the quality of life for any society is, in large part, determined by the level of education of its citizenry. The citizenry is the body that establishes laws and governs, that operates the businesses, that creates jobs, that educates, that operates the health care industries, that provides safety and security, and that ensures the overall quality of life of the community. If the citizenry is not educated, trained, or skilled, what is the future for the quality of life in the community? Given the current issues in education, it is apparent that significant numbers of future adults, many of whom are already marginalized, will be ill-equipped to fill critical roles in society if significant changes are not made in the mindsets and skill sets of the students to empower them to excel in extraordinary ways and in diverse fields of study. If the masses are not educated, who will perform the critical tasks of society?

Imagine the Ideal School

Have you ever thought about what the ideal school would look like? Imagine children who are happy, energetic, and focused on learning coming into the school house eager and ready to learn as they prepare to interact with their peers locally, nationally, and internationally in twenty-first-century digitally equipped classrooms. Imagine joyously exuberant teachers standing at the doorway to their classrooms, ready and eager to greet each student by name and with a smile and prepared to begin the lessons for the day with a variety of intellectually-stimulating teaching tools to engage students and to facilitate student learning. As each class starts, imagine that students already know exactly what the instructional objectives and learning outcomes will be, and they excitedly choose from multiple options to achieve the learning outcomes. Imagine the learning experiences being contextualized and structured so that all students can relate to the relevancy of the lesson in their personal lives. Imagine students raising their hands to answer teachers' questions about the lesson and then periodically referring to their smart technology tools to research the history of concepts and then putting their chairs in circles of learning communities to discuss solutions to problems that affect their locales and the larger global community. At the end of every class, imagine students thanking the teachers for a great lesson and reluctantly leaving the classroom because of the positive energy generated and the significant lessons learned. Finally, imagine students and teachers ending the school day with a great deal of satisfaction at the outcomes, and eager for a new school day to begin.

This description is simple, and it is ideal because it describes a setting where children and teachers want to spend their time. It describes an environment where learning is active, where children are motivated, where teachers are properly credentialed, and where the school is equipped with the proper technology and other tools to engage students in a 21st century learning experience everyday.

Looking retrospectively, the African American slaves knew the value of education and risked their lives to attain an education for themselves and for their children. They knew that education could be life transforming. For generations, societal and institutional restrictions and limitations were placed upon what individuals, depending upon their race or gender, could learn, where they could pursue their learning, and how they could use their new knowledge, talent, and skills. Today, the opportunities for young African Americans to complete a public high school education is state-supported and also supported by taxpayers; yet the hunger and zeal for an education seem to pale in comparison to that hunger and zeal described by Booker T. Washington in his book, *Up From Slavery*. The conditions then were less than accommodating, yet the freed slaves had an unrivaled passion and thirst to learn. People endured the worst of human conditions and the extreme of sacrifices to attain an education. What has happened over the years to dampen that zeal? Can it be restored? The answer is, yes it can.

During the years of slavery and for generations thereafter, there have been glass ceilings that limited the upward mobility of African Americans. Despite the tremendous strides toward equality realized in the twenty-first century, the educational glass ceiling still exists today. The foremost area wherein the glass ceiling still exists today is in the glass ceiling of each person's mind, whether child or teacher, that imposes limitations upon them. The glass ceiling can be obliterated forever through a new order of thinking. The new order is an educational process that allows all students to believe they can optimize their potential and that provides every teacher with the essential tools.

Practitioners have found that diverse teaching strategies advance student learning. One example includes contextual learning which involves hands-on approaches to education. The contextual learning may include internship experiences for students and service learning projects. Internships also provide great experiences for students to engage in work and research experiences. Service learning is usually a part of the academic experience that the student is engaged in at the time and promotes learning through a cycle of action and reflection. In service learning, students usually work on a team with others to apply what they are learning to address community problems. During their times of reflection, they can develop their cognitive skills by thinking through the totality of their experiences. No doubt, from all observations, service learning helps build leadership skills, character, and a sense of responsibility.

A CALL TO ACTION

Some of the common characteristics that researchers describe in African American children include low self-concept, low self-respect, and negative group identification. Research studies also indicate that African American students are more field dependent and white students are more field independent. Field-dependent students are influenced by their immediate environment; they prefer to work in groups and relate to information in a social context. Field-independent students, on the other hand, are not dependent upon their specific environment, are more interested in working alone, and are task oriented. On the intellectual domain of black and white students, no differences were identified; however, there were differences in the social and perceptual areas for African American children which confirms the need for practitioners to focus on these areas, the social and the perceptual, in working with African American children to enhance their academic success.

In many instances, the crisis in public education today is a people problem. When people are not aware of the cultural and subcultural differences or when they ignore the differences, problems can arise. But these differences point to indicators about how individuals perceive themselves and the world around them, what they value, and how the pedagogy may be designed to help them learn. It is true that it takes a village to raise a child. Today, it also takes a village to educate a child. That is particularly true for many African American children who grow up in urban environments and under impoverished conditions that limit their opportunities. "It takes a village to raise a child" is an African proverb prominently used in the Nigerian Igbo culture. "*Ora Na Azu Nwa*" which means it takes the community/village to raise a child. The Igbos also name their children *nwa ora*, which means child of the community. According to research, this reference is typical in many African tribes and not singularly attributable to the Igbo.

In the United States, there are so many brilliant minds that can be saved by groups collaborating together to educate, to mentor, and to support the healthy development of African American children. Many groups today are serving in that capacity through Big Brothers and Sisters, the YMCA and YWCA, African American fraternities and sororities, the Urban League, the National Association for the Advancement of Colored People, Parent Teacher Organizations, churches, ministerial alliances, and others are rallying to the call to assist the schools to enrich the educational experiences of African American youth. This is what is needed. The net should be broadened to ensure that every student succeeds and that *No child is Left Behind* as emphasized in former President George W. Bush's administration and that no child is denied a quality education.

Society has changed in so many ways, but most things about the educational system have remained static. Think about the dramatic change that has occurred as society has shifted from an agrarian economy to a computerized, knowledge-based economy. The infrastructure and technology have changed as those shifts have occurred. Evidence of those shifts are apparent with old tools either being eliminated due to obsolescence or to old tools being refined or even retrofitted due to the changing technology. Many educational institutions, however, still function as they did during the pre-computer age: seat time as a standard for knowledge acquisition, many classrooms being confined to physical spaces, and twelve years of schooling being required to complete a high school diploma.

The next several chapters present a Learning for Ownership (LO) Typology and Empowerment Model that position teachers and students as joint partners for student success. The Learning for Ownership Typology presents the characteristics and traits among most students, and the empowerment model presents a process that can be integrated into the curriculum to prepare more African American students for success.

Introducing the Learning for Ownership Typology for African American Student Success

The objective of this chapter is to introduce a typology that describes seven distinct attitudinal/behavioral types among many youth in Pre-K through 12th grade schools. The typology is provided to help teachers intervene with students to identify and address problems that often interfere with students' overall performance and persistency in school. This section, to use an agrarian metaphor, will seed change into the lives of teachers and students. Well, you might ask, "How will you do that?" I will do that with a descriptive process that identifies, sorts, and analyzes attitudinal and behaviorial profiles. Seeding change is what this and succeeding chapters will provide. Like my grandfather, the master farmer and businessman, whom I referenced in a previous chapter, I believe the crops that you grow are really responsive to the seeds that you sow. When grandfather wanted to grow corn, he planted corn seed. When he wanted cotton, he planted cotton seed. Neither crop just sprang up accidentally. Good, healthy crops required time, effort, and attentiveness. They still do. He had to prepare the soil, till the field, plant the seed, water the soil, chop away the weeds, and then gather the harvest. He handled his crops with care, ensuring that he used the proper and the best fertilizers to ward off pests and insects of various kinds that could potentially destroy his investment. Occasionally, he would position a scarecrow in the field to keep the birds from eating his tender crops. While children are not the same as cotton or corn, figurataively speaking, they are our investment; thus, the preparation process, the tilling process, and the weeding and feeding processes all apply until the children are fully developed physically, mentally, and intellectually. In the end analysis, as the harvested crops provide sustenance for the masses, well-educated students will provide value through an improved quality of life for the community. And just as the scarecrows kept the birds at bay, the parents and extended family members must be vigilant in advocating fairness, quality, and equity for their children to keep dream killers at bay.

In previous chapters, I discussed the role and purpose of education and the essential components of what matters in urban education to improve students' receptivity to learning. I identified the main issues interfering with African American children's view of school and their persistency in school and stated the case for improving the quality and delivery of education to African American children. Finally, I concluded with research findings from studies on African American children that substantiated that the primary factors affecting the children are sociocultural: self-esteem issues, perceptual issues, and negative race identification. There was not evidence nor was there a finding to support the long-held suspicion that African American children are uneducable or unwilling to learn. Also, the conclusion from research on the brain confirmed that "a child can learn as long as the natural processes are not interrupted." Thus, the primary problems for African American children stem from their self-image, their belief system, their experiential system, and their preconditioning even before they arrive at school.

Certainly, schools must be actively involved in identifying and correcting the problems that inhibit children's ability to learn. Parents and the extended village, on the other hand, have a fundamental role to play in the Pre-K through 12th grade years to address the sociocultural issues that affect self-esteem, self-perception, and perception of others. In part, this can be accomplished by speaking positive affirmations to children that will cultivate strong, positive self-images. Much of what is construed as negative racial identification and negative self-image is learned in the home or among friends during the preschool years. For example, I have heard some parents use derogatory terms when talking to their children. I have also heard some children use pejorative terms and negative references when referring to each other. This type of behavior is insidious. It creates the mindset even before the children enroll in school about their image, what they believe about themselves, and what they believe about others who look like them. This attitude can spawn other negative attitudes, become entrenched, and continue throughout life. It can, in fact, ruin a person's life.

Negative, disparaging language should never be used in school either, especially with young children. I have, for years, heard young African American children called at risk, uneducable, lazy, no good, bad, and many other terms that berate and undermine them. Some of the references are so belittling that I have seen children literally cry. The hurtful effects are more severe when teachers use the demeaning language because they are typically thought to be more sensitive to others and more responsible in what they say. When teachers disappoint students by using harsh references, the children can become easily disillusioned. So what happens from that point when students believe the negative reports? The script that describes the prophecy escalates in the following manner. The children arrive at school and act out. The teachers and the principal meet with the children and affirm the following: "You are bad. You are a troublemaker. You are destructive." Or the students would be required to sit in a corner, facing the wall, with a dunce cap on their heads. At the extreme, students would be suspended or expelled from school. Depending upon the perspective, perhaps the dunce cap is the worst of all options for young boys. After all, what decent young girl would entertain conversations with a boy who was humiliated by having to sit on a stool while facing a corner with a dunce cap on his head? So, given the treatment that some students experience, it is no wonder that they drop out. Others commit acts that lead to their suspension or expulsion. Research studies show that in 1999, 35 percent of African American students in grades seven through twelve had been suspended or expelled during their school years, compared to 13 percent of Asians and 15 percent of whites. Do you think early interventions could have prevented the chain reaction of problems? In the end analysis, it is no wonder that more African American high school students are falling behind their white counterparts in graduation rates, academic achievement rates, literacy rates, and college preparedness rates. It is no wonder that in the doll studies, the African American children identified the black doll as the bad child and as the ugly child and the white doll as the good child and the attractive child. In part, they are told this in their homes and in their associations with friends; they see the preferences in magazines, in newspapers, and on television. Many of them believe this, so how are African American children to think and act differently without proper interventions?

As Dr. Asa Hilliard said and was referenced earlier, "Students are always learning: good, bad, or indifferent, and teachers are always teaching: good, bad, or indifferent." So, while some African American children are being told of their insignificance, the white children, for the most part, are being told of their great value. And for many white children, it is likely that their parents are using terms of endearment and affirming language to cultivate strong, positive young men and women. "You will be powerful, just like your dad." "You are a child prodigy." "You are a good child. You are intelligent. You can become anything that you want to become. There are no restrictions on your life." Even when the verbal language is not spoken, the children can see in their physical surroundings images that establish their beliefs. Consequently, like the black children, the white children believe the early messages they hear and receive from the people in their environment, and they often act accordingly.

Sociocultural factors represent one set of circumstances for African American children to overcome. This challenge, in and of itself, can be daunting. Now couple that set of issues with another set of academic-readiness issues that are said to be predictive of student success. This coupling of sociocultural issues with academic-readiness issues creates enormous educational gaps and pressures even before the children enroll in school. As you recall from the previous chapter, it was found that "four of the five greatest predictors of eventual success at a college or university are applied and achieved before a child even enters school." Those factors are the quantity and quality of discussion in the child's home, the clarity of value systems, strong peer group support, and the amount of independent reading. What attitudes and emotions do you think emerge when children enter school grappling with fundamental issues that challenge them psychologically on one hand and academically on the other? This coupling leads to false assumptions that African American children are not as smart as others when the truth is that socioeconomic conditions, in this instance, are defining the experiences and opportunities of the children based upon either their fortune or misfortune pertaining to their parents' socio-economic status.

This chapter presents the Learning for Ownership Typology that classifies the attitudes that emerge from the negative sociocultural conditioning, the negative race identification, the negative self-image and self-esteem that African American children experience. The intent is —like my grandfather, the master farmer, would contend—to chop away the weeds that threaten their future and introduce a support system designed to cultivate a healthy and plentiful harvest. I contend that the academic achievement of the children cannot be fully addressed until the psychosocial issues that paralyze the children emotionally and academically are adequately resolved. Learning for Ownership is a contribution to that process.

Learning for Ownership: What Is It?

Learning for Ownership is an empowerment model to enhance African American student success. It involves three components: 1) identifying and classifying students' personal attitudinal profiles, 2) examining and validating students' experiences, thoughts, and beliefs, and 3) creating an ownership culture that links entrepreneurial principles and practices to achievable goals. In effect, Learning for Ownership allows the practitioner to help students through behavioral modification and by eliminating the bad and replacing it with good. This means eliminating the destructive attitudes, destructive behaviors, bad choices, and bad thinking and replacing those with constructive attitudes, constructive behaviors, and proper choices and thoughts. As an outcome of Learning for Ownership, students should readily embrace the fact that they are the owners of everything they do in and with their lives. They own their ability to make choices. They own their hopes and dreams or lack thereof. They own everything that they learn or choose not to learn. They are the responsible agents for everything that they choose to happen in their lives, for they are the owners of their lives. What they do with it is determined by them.

Following is the Learning for Ownership Typology that classifies the most common behaviors and tendencies that I have observed in African American children over the past thirty years. The Learning for Ownership Typology is a tool that teachers and counselors can utilize to identify student profiles that open the door to more constructive conversations that will facilitate self-improvement and change. The categories are as follows. Stage one is the attitude of anger. Stage two is the attitude of apathy. Stage three is the attitude of skepticism. Stage four is the player's attitude. Stage five is the dreamer's attitude. Stage six is the realist's attitude. Stage seven is the achiever's attitude. I believe that each of the attitudes is a manifestation, in different forms, of the overarching problem that plagues many African American children: low self esteem, negative race identification, and socio-cultural conditioning. I further believe that most African American children have experienced several of the stages depending upon the events in their lives. Finally, I believe that all students can become consistent achievers, which is the preferred stage. If teachers and counselors know the stage that students are operating in at the moment, they are better equipped to intervene when children are displaying aberrant behaviors and properly correct the problem.

Stage One: The Attitude of Anger

Anger is not a unique emotion to a specific race, ethnic group, age, or gender. Most individuals have experienced anger. Anger usually occurs when a person feels wronged in some way, treated unfairly or disrespectfully, or when he or she does not get what is expected. When there is a barrage of negative experiences that occurs on a regular basis, particularly when a person has low self-esteem, anger becomes a likely emotion that leads to behavioral problems.

These emotions do not escape children, and some come into the classroom with behaviors and attitudes that reflect their anger. As a former public school educator, there were many instances where I witnessed children talking disrespectfully to adults, getting into arguments and fights with their classmates, and displaying acts of defiance. On a few occasions, the students would disrupt the classroom instruction with inappropriate outbursts that showed their defiance. All of these acts were, in fact, based upon the unresolved anger that had percolated inside the students. Many educational practitioners have seen the vast range of student emotions and have addressed the problems to the best of their ability. In talking to educators about their experiences with students, one teacher shared her distress about the students who are frequently sent to the principal's office due to their inappropriate behavior or their acts of defiance. Sometimes the students are self-destructive. One student had tried to glue his eyelids together. Another had tried to staple his lips together. In another instance, the student was hostile and did not understand the cause of his anger until the teacher initiated a conversation with the student to identify the source of the problem. Once the problem was identified, it caused a 180-degree shift in the student's attitude and behavior. The student admitted to being angry because his dad was in jail; his mother was struggling financially; and he, as the oldest child, had the burden of helping the family make ends meet until the dad returned. Once the source of his anger was identified, the student said he felt relieved and was better able to cope with the demands of home and school. In another instance, a colleague commented to me about a child in her classroom who would often curse when he got excited or frustrated. The teacher did not understand the basis of the sudden outbursts until parent-teacher night when the parents visited the school. In conversation with the parents, the teacher discussed the child's outbursts and indicated that this behavior was a recurring problem. The dad became agitated, the teacher said, and quipped, "That little (expletive deleted). I'll fix his little (expletive deleted) when I get home." Suddenly, the teacher knew the source of the child's problem.

Talking to students and helping them identify the source of their anger and helping them overcome their feelings and attitudes is essential to resolving the problems. For those who express their emotions because they believe they have not been dealt a fair hand in life or that they are not being treated fairly, they become angry and sometimes act out those feelings. According to the profile, the angry student is usually upset because of his perception of being wronged or hurt and therefore retaliates. At some point, the angry student could strike out randomly at others due to the multiple negative factors that impact his life. It could be that nothing has gone well in this student's life; the home life could be in turmoil, and the student could be the object of negative feedback and put-downs by friends. The student looks at people around him and sees everyone else who looks just like him in dire straits. This type of student is angry because of his or her circumstances. There is no place where the angry person feels at peace for long. He is angry. He walks around as though he is ready to explode. In the end analysis, the student looks in the mirror and starts seeing everything bad that everyone else says they see when they look at him.

As a high school teacher, I saw the bitterness and the rage that some students carried like an albatross. As a young teacher, I did not have the savvy to address the problem and was not prepared in my educational classes or in my practicums to do anything more than send the student to the principal's office.

That approach did not rectify the problem in my classroom. In fact, it created more of a cloud for the students and uncertainty for me as I prepared to teach. I remember teaching one lesson about the Civil War and making a factual statement as cited in the textbook about President Abraham Lincoln. One African American student in the class became so upset that he initially lashed out and then started crying as he emphatically articulated his admiration of President Lincoln and how he personally knew that the president's primary objective was to free the slaves, not to save the Union as the author of the text had indicated. I never talked to the student to learn the source of his rage, particularly about an event that occurred generations before his birth; however, I was very careful from that point forward how I presented information even from the text to avoid unwittingly inciting students. This student, like several others, walked around with his fists clenched as though he was prepared to strike someone at any moment. Sometimes, of course, some students are mentally unstable, and that case is one that should be recognized and immediately referred to the counselor or to the health care professional.

The suppressed anger that a student has is perhaps the most unsettling. This is the outwardly mild-mannered person who appears to be quiet and easygoing but is near the boiling point inside with anger and resentment. The practitioner has an opportunity to learn about the children and hear their emotions that explain their attitudes once the opportunity for conversation is opened to them.

It is important in either instance of the anger, whether expressed or suppressed, for that emotion to be identified and to be focused into a more positive direction.

As a teacher, it was intimidating to have angry students in the class. I had seen them in their moments of rage and thought it prudent to consider what-if scenarios in the event an in-class situation escalated out of control. Often, the anger that students displayed could be detected in their nonverbal behavior (body language and facial expressions, as well as the verbal language they would sometimes use). That was always a clue for me. Since I could not anticipate what the student might do at any given point in time, I chose to be very careful in an effort to avoid offending or creating a tipping point for the angry student. This I thought was necessary for several reasons: the police never walked the school corridors, my classroom was quite a distance from the main office, the intercom was only a one-way communication device from the principal's office, and I did not have a way to protect myself and twenty-nine other persons who were in my class. So I was on my own with thirty students every class period. If an altercation had occurred, I would not have been able to subdue and control the situation without backup support. The classroom safety and security measures for teachers are not so vastly different today.

The angry students are the ones who are most in need of professional counseling – in part due to their unresolved issues and their potential harm to others and to themselves. I recall vivid examples of students who were angry because their parents' financial status would not allow them to have the same types of trendy clothing as their peers. Today, many schools in urban communities have addressed this problem through a uniform dress code by which all children must abide. This simple change has leveled the playing field in those schools for all children and has, no doubt, reduced the anxiety and frustration for children who suffer from negative self-images.

Stage Two: The Attitude of Apathy

It sounds insulting, but yes, there are students who have apathetic attitudes. The reference is not intended to further demoralize students. Their attitudes are caused by stimuli in their environment and can, with effort, be alleviated. Colleagues who work as teachers in large, urban communities frequently address the apathy that students display. It reflects an attitude that suggests that they have given up on life.

Apathy is an attitude that some students experience as a result of low self-esteem, negative race identification, socio-cultural conditioning, and poor perceptual feelings. I have concluded that the student experiencing apathy does not feel good about himself or about others and does not feel that he can do anything to change his circumstances, so his attitude is, "Why bother?" and, "Why worry?" This student type is the one that is totally indifferent and shows little or no emotion. He does not care if he is in school or out of school. Nothing matters. This is the student who will go along with anyone because he really does not care. If you ask the student a series of questions, the answers will always be with the shrug of the shoulder or the common rejoinder, "I don't know, and I don't care." Nothing seems to arouse the passion of students experiencing apathy. The students learn apathy from their parents, peers, or from personal experiences where they tried to accomplish goals but were unsuccessful. So they developed the attitude, "What will be will be." They see the behaviors in their homes and hear the comments made by adults, so they pattern after them. Unfortunately, the apathetic students feel powerless to change their circumstances. The common statements that I heard follow. "Why go to school? You won't get a good job anyway." "Why argue? People will do what they want to anyway." Then, to add insult to injury, the students recite the examples that support their point of view. For example, they remember the young man in the neighborhood who completed a college degree and is now driving a taxicab or the young woman who finished high school but was not accepted into a local university. These are the kinds of examples they use to support their attitudes. These individuals feel, first and foremost, that they are powerless to change their lives and their circumstances. It is apparent that the conditions of life have totally overwhelmed them, and they are not motivated to do anything to change the circumstances. Apathy sets in instead of the anger to which some of the students resort. Students who are experiencing apathy have said to me that they are often ignored in school and feel that they are discriminated against by their teachers. Then, they retort that it is fine with them because no amount of attention from the teachers will make a difference anyway. If this feeling enroots, then the perception becomes reality for them and the manifestations of that attitude follow in the form of poor homework, late homework, and sloppy homework that the teacher marks with failing grades. At this point, the student begins to believe that the apathy is justified.

Stage Three: The Attitude of Skepticism

The skeptic questions everything. Skepticism can develop when a person has low self-esteem, negative race identification, and negative sociocultural and perceptual perspectives. The skeptic questions every motive and often misses out on great opportunities due to his mistrust of others. Many times, this attitude develops early in a child's life through countless disappointments with loved ones and those who make promises that are not kept or those who disappoint them in other ways by saying one thing yet doing another thing that conflicts. The skeptic is not apathetic; he is just cautious. The sociocultural conditioning is often the reason for the skeptic's behavior. Unlike the student with apathy, who does not care, the skeptic might care too much because he always questions and challenges every action and everything without any factual basis to justify his skepticism.

Stage Four: The Attitude of the Player

The player could almost be considered the joker. He is always fun loving, pulling pranks, and is the life of the party. The problem, however, is that the joker is sad inside and is overcompensating in order to hide his sadness. The player is the joker; he is the one to be the class clown. When the lights go out, the player returns to his quiet state that is next to depression. For some students, acting out the role of a player is a survival mechanism. This is the face they put on to hide all of the pain and sadness they feel in their everyday lives, so they pretend. Students who have demonstrated characteristics of the player have the ability to succeed if they could be transplanted from the environment they are in to a healthier environment. Some have theorized that a boarding school concept for bright African American children would be a great way to temporarily remove them from their impoverished living conditions in an effort to give them a better chance in life. The player would be a primary candidate for a learning environment that is holistic, safe, and nurturing.

Stage Five: The Attitude of the Dreamer

Students respond variously to negative race identification, issues that cause some to experience low self-esteem and low sociocultural and perceptual problems. In fact, those factors do not deter dreamers. Dreamers are fixated on ways to improve their lives and their circumstances, so they begin to dream about the big house, the luxurious automobile, the fabulous clothes, and all of the material possessions that money can buy. The dreamer often does not understand the full range of career opportunities that is available, so he dreams about the limited opportunities that he knows about. Dreamers often limit their aspirations to acquiring material possessions without developing an acceptable plan to achieve them. And the question becomes, "Is the dreamer willing to do whatever it takes to attain material possessions?" Some see the shortcut solutions to achieving their goals. Others might pursue education, but they do not comprehend the educational pathways that lead to career success. This statement is particularly true of many African American children. They are limited in their knowledge, information, and understanding about career pathways to success. They see positive role models, yet they do not understand the steps required to attain the same level or to enter the same profession. What I have discovered is that many students who initially lack information about career opportunities become excited about the pursuit once they know the particulars: the pathways, the time frame to completion, and the income potential.

The dreamer's inability to achieve his goal could lead to one of the previously described attitudes: anger, apathy, or skepticism. Therefore, it is important that practitioners provide students with information that guides them to make sound decisions and to pursue goal attainment. The problem of the dreamer was made ever clearer to me when my husband, an associate juvenile court judge, and I were speaking to a group of young people who were part of a special after-school initiative for juvenile offenders. The audience was comprised of twenty-five young African American and Hispanic men and women, all of them between the ages of fourteen and eighteen. During that session, the fork-in-the-road moment occurred when I asked the students about their personal goals in life and their career aspirations. They all stared at us as though there was suddenly a breakdown in communication. There was a long, pregnant pause. It was clear they had no idea what they wanted to become. Finally, one said that he wanted to become an NBA star, to which all the others nodded in agreement. When we asked him the steps to becoming an NBA star, he and all of the other students were stumped. When we asked what he was doing to achieve his goal, he was silenced. Students should be encouraged to dream without succumbing to what Langston Hughes identifies in his poem as a dream deferred? The final questions Hughes asks in his poem are, "What happens to a dream deferred...does it dry up like a raisin in the sun? Or does it explode?" Neither is a good outcome. It is important that the practical steps to attaining the dream are identified so the dream can be realized. The dreamers know what they want; they do not know all of the how-to steps to achieve their dreams. That is where the practitioners must play a vital role to help the dreamers look beyond their present circumstances to envision future possibilities.

Stage Six: The Attitude of the Realist

The realist is also a person who does not allow the negative race identification or other sociocultural issues to impede his pursuit of education. The realist is the student who knows what he wants to become and knows what is required to achieve his goal. The realist understands the behaviors and attitudes of other individuals and sees the world as it truly exists. He knows there will be obstacles of various kinds, but he also knows that it is his prerogative to decide how he handles the obstacles in his life. So, once again, it is the family of the realist who indicates to the child that if you want to get ahead in life, you had better get an education. You had better try to get all of the knowledge that you can in an effort to create value for yourself. They decry those who demonstrate anger, apathy, skepticism, or other negative attitudes. They believe that the onus is on each person to make of life what he will without blame or anger being directed at others for failings or shortcomings.

It is clear that many of the freed slaves, even given their horrendous circumstances, were realists. They could have been angry or apathetic, but they saw life as it was and knew that if they were to improve their lives and the lives of their children that education would be necessary. Therefore, they chose the struggle for education.

Stage Seven: The Attitude of the Achiever

The achiever has a positive self-concept despite his conditions in life. He is the student who has developed a renewed mindset, so while he might temporarily live in substandard housing, the substandard housing does not define who he is and what he will become. The achiever has made a quality decision to improve his skill sets in order to be successful in life. He is confident, loyal to family and friends, and applies the highest ethical standards in all decisions. He has a healthy sense of life and of how to achieve goals. The achiever knows that success flows from many channels; therefore, he builds quality relationships with others; he develops his intellect,and he sharpens his skills and competencies. This person is purposeful and is conscientious about his image and his overall presentation to others. He represents the ideal model encompassing realistic views of the world, an honest assessment of himself and others, and a drive and determination to achieve his goals in life.

The achiever has resolved that he will not allow the circumstances of life to impact him. The achiever is absolutely determined to achieve his goals and will not allow what he considers to be trivial matters to interfere. This is the individual who has dogged determination and holds firmly to the conviction that no matter what, he will achieve his goals. His attitude toward the insults from others is like the witticism that says, "Sticks and stones may break my bones, but words will never harm me."

ANALYSIS OF THE TYPOLOGY

Throughout my years as an educator, I have found the distinct types identified in the typology to be rather precise and the classifications to be rather accurate. I hypothesize that the social ills presented earlier (sociocultural conditioning, negative race identification, low self esteem, low perceptual images) will influence the students' dispositions as reflected in their responses to the typology. In many instances, the family members feel unqualified to provide counsel and advice other than offering encouraging words that remind the children to stay in school and get a good education. No doubt, a strategic support system is needed to guide students through the process of goal attainment.

As referenced earlier, most African American students are not acquainted with the vast availability of educational and career pathways. I witnessed the transformation that occurred with inner-city students who were involved in a school-to-careers program that, in effect, groomed them for educational success. Students enjoyed the benefits of career orientations, career counseling, field trips to college and university campuses, opportunities to shadow business professionals, and the opportunity to establish a small business start-up in the high school to manage and operate a small newspaper. For many students, this opportunity raised their consciousness and helped raise the expectations in their lives. What was clear to me was that a broad network of support was available to help promote student success: educators, business and civic leaders, parents, and other major stakeholders. Thus, this is where the village is required to help as stakeholders to mentor and provide career information and outreach opportunities for students.

As I conclude this chapter, some people might say, "Well, this is another tool to stereotype students." It is not. It is a learning for ownership tool to help teachers work more confidently with students. In review, the teacher will learn to identify the profiles and establish educational experiences to restructure the thoughts of students who exhibit characteristics of one of the seven stages on the Typology. So, the first phase of the Typology is used to identify and classify attitudes and behaviors. The second phase is a tool for behavioral modification, and the third phase is a plan for student self actualization. Now, let us further explore a tool that practitioners can utilize to work with their students in a proactive way to help them overcome the psychosocial issues that currently interfere with their self-esteem, their performance in school, and their ultimate success in life.

The Learning for Ownership Profile and Survey

This chapter provides the tools for teachers and counselors to use to identify and classify students' attitudinal perspectives and behaviors. It also provides a tool for teachers to use with students to begin the behavioral modification process. The profile is created for the teacher's use as a quick reference guide to common behaviors and attitudes that interfere with student learning. The list is not exhaustive, so teachers may discover other important behaviors to add to the list. For example, if a child has consistently missed several days of class and then returns to school, the teacher should highlight that concern on the profile and request that the counselor visit with the student to ascertain whether there is a problem that the school can help address. Many schools have truant officers; but these persons, while serving an important function, are often viewed as adversaries rather than as advocates, and their jobs are really quite different from that of a teacher or a counselor. Therefore, the truant officers would not be the best agents to follow up with students about a meeting where academic support and encouragement would be provided. As a part of the meeting, the counselor should, at some point, request that the student complete the Learning for Ownership Survey. The student's responses to the survey will allow the counselor to examine with the student his responses and discuss any attitudinal or behavioral issues highlighted in the survey that could impede the student's success. Learning for Ownership should be discussed with the student as an empowerment process to improve and enrich his life.

As you recall, the Learning for Ownership Typology identifies seven classifications of attitudinal responses that often result from negative race identification, negative sociocultural conditioning, and negative perceptual issues. These sociocultural factors serve as a springboard that spiral into other degenerating experiences that further complicate students' lives. This chapter provides a profile of each of the categories in the typology. The classifications are discrete; they are not hierarchical or progressive which would suggest that a person ascends from one category to the next. The discrete categories are provided, followed by a student survey and comments from focus groups.

As you will see, the Learning for Ownership Profile and Survey, allow teachers and counselors to work together in an early alert mode to detect potential problems and to implement support systems for students. It is recommended that the profile and all information pertaining to it be used in accordance with the school district's policies and procedures and in accordance with all federal, state, and local guidelines that apply to student privacy.

As every teacher knows, student behaviors are already labeled and put into categories, if not on paper, in the minds of practitioners. So, when the practitioners see certain children, they automatically categorize them based upon previous experiences, hearsay, or perceptions. Usually, this occurs without practitioners taking the next steps to confirm and, if necessary, rectify attitudes and behaviors before a crisis develops.

Nevertheless, teachers know what their assignments entail, pedagogically, to instruct the children. Counselors also know what their assignments entail in performing guidance functions. Currently, teachers and counselors work in separate silos to perform their duties. The Learning for Ownership process, however, requires a team of advocates with teachers and counselors working together as a frontline support team for student success. Their working collaboratively will allow them to respond with a higher degree of precision and accountability to identify and ameliorate student problems. In the role of advocate for student success, teachers and counselors should be visible early on in the academic year to inform students of their services and to provide assistance.

To my surprise, many students indicate that they are not familiar with the vast array of services that counseling departments provide and unfortunately do not seek counseling support independently. As a result of the limited information about available resources, many students who could benefit from counseling support do not seek help.

HELP IS AVAILABLE TO THE SCHOOLS

A tremendous resource that many schools overlook is the African American church to assist schools when student-oriented issues arise. Separation of church and state laws limit the partnership; but the reality is that for many African Americans, the church is still the dominant center of influence in the black community. In many African American communities, the church is viewed as an advocate to help each person live a fulfilled life. Thus, it would be advantageous for public schools to form a partnership with African American churches, within the confines of the law, to help mentor the youth.

So, in addition to students having attitudinal issues that they are grappling with, the public schools that they are attending are also suffering from image problems and the stigma of being identified as failing schools. If you stop for a moment, you can understand some of the students' aberrant behaviors even though the behaviors are unacceptable. Consider these questions: How do you respond to people who try to undermine and demean you? How do you interact with individuals who are brusque and authoritative? When you are seeking a service and the attendant insults you, how do you respond? Human nature is all the same, whether for adults or for young people. Reciprocity in behavior that applies the Golden Rule is essential.

In the previous chapter, I discussed the stages of the Learning for Ownership Typology. Now, I will provide a snapshot of each stage. The profile provides a quick and easy checklist for teachers to classify the students' attitudes and behaviors.

Learning for Ownership Profile

A Checklist of Student Attitudes and Behaviors

Profile: Behaviors/Dates:

Instructions: Check the attitudes and behaviors that apply to your class. Write notes and keep dates of all incidences.

Profile One

Frequent outbursts
Nonverbal gestures that depict anger
Acts of defiance
Altercations with others
Self-destructive behaviors
Argumentative
Aggression toward others
Threatens others
Holds grudges

Revengeful
Resentful
Loud
Boisterous
Antagonistic

Profile Two

Laid back
Quiet
Indifferent
Does not seem to care about anything or anyone
Lethargic
Says school is a waste of time
Shows little or no emotion
Submits sloppy homework

Profile Three

Questions everything
Doubts everything
Critical of everything and everyone
Does not make commitments
Untrusting
Suspicious
Does not believe until they have checked things out for themselves

Profile Four

The joker (Joking in a cynical or mean way because of anger or joking as a reflection of the personality)
Happy-go-lucky
Playful

The life of the party
Always on stage
The actor
The comedian
Fun loving

Profile Five

Day dreamer
Has a big vision but no plan to achieve
Fantasizes
Reacts without thinking
Vivid imagination
Lives in his dreams
Out of touch with reality
Spontaneous

Profile Six

Has a healthy view of life and goals
Well grounded
Does not take anyone or anything for granted
Accepts the world as it is and deals with it
Accepts responsibility
Accepts consequences of actions
Self Reliant
Practical
Exercises good judgment

Profile Seven

Serious
Goal-oriented
Attentive
Critical Thinker

Conscientious about getting work done on time
Has a positive self-concept
Has high self-esteem
Believes he can achieve
Committed
Determined
Broad network of support
Always marketing self
 Self-confident

Categorically speaking, it is not just the children who have negative attitudinal problems. There are some educators who also fall into some of the categories identified; that topic will not be discussed at this time but will be discussed very briefly in a later chapter.

Following is a companion tool to the profile that is called "What Is My Attitude Today?" This survey is for students to help highlight their attitudes in a broad range of areas. It is intended to serve as a guage to help students clarify their feelings and to seek support from their team of advocates.

A Survey Tool for Students

///

What Is My Attitude Today?
A Learning for Ownership Student Support Questionnaire

Following is a list of statements that reflects how you feel about people, events, circumstances, and even yourself. There are no right or wrong answers, so you can relax and be honest in your responses. This information will be used in a confidential and constructive way to assist you on your journey to becoming empowered through the Learning for Ownership Empowerment Process. Simply respond to each statement by marking either of the numbers, 1 through 5, that most reflects how you feel. As an example, if there were a statement that says, "I am people oriented," I would mark my response in the box that is number 5, which indicates "Always," because I enjoy interacting with individuals and with groups of people. Since this survey is not timed, please take your time to complete it as honestly as possible. Be sure to stop and ask the counselor for clarification if you have a question.

1=Never, 2=Seldom, 3=Sometimes, 4=Most of the time, 5=Always

I am a very happy and outgoing person.

1   2   3   4   5

I enjoy making friends with different types of people.

1   2   3   4   5

I am happy with who I am.

1   2   3   4   5

I wish I were a different complexion.

1   2   3   4   5

I get uncontrollably upset about things that happen to me.

1   2   3   4   5

I think my education will help me get a good job.

1   2   3   4   5

I enjoy my home life.

1   2   3   4   5

I enjoy spending time with my family.

1   2   3   4   5

I help people who are in need.

1   2   3   4   5

I enjoy spending time with friends.

1   2   3   4   5

I am a positive person.

1   2   3   4   5

I think I can make a difference in the world.

1   2   3   4   5

I think my race gives me an advantage.

        1   2   3   4   5

I am proud to be the person that I am.

        1   2   3   4   5

I agree with the slogan, "Black is beautiful."

        1   2   3   4   5

I choose friends who look just like me.

        1   2   3   4   5

I am happy with my family life.

        1   2   3   4   5

I prefer teachers who are of my race.

        1   2   3   4   5

I believe the way I look defines me.

        1   2   3   4   5

I try to change the way I look.

        1   2   3   4   5

I enjoy school.

        1   2   3   4   5

I respect my teachers.

        1   2   3   4   5

I am treated fairly at school

        1   2   3   4   5

I get angry quite often.

        1   2   3   4   5

I have been told that I have a chip on my shoulder.

        1   2   3   4   5

I hide my emotions when I get angry.

       1   2   3   4   5

I express my anger instead of holding it in.

       1   2   3   4   5

I feel like I'm always on the defensive.

       1   2   3   4   5

I am a nonchalant person.

       1   2   3   4   5

I like to just drift through life.

       1   2   3   4   5

I believe the saying "What will be will be."

       1   2   3   4   5

I believe people should just relax and let life take its course.

       1   2   3   4   5

I believe nobody really cares about me.

       1   2   3   4   5

I just like to coast through life.

       1   2   3   4   5

I try not to have feelings about anything.

       1   2   3   4   5

I question what people tell me.

       1   2   3   4   5

I second-guess myself.

       1   2   3   4   5

I joke around with people to have fun.

       1   2   3   4   5

I like to make people laugh.

    1   2   3   4   5

I use jokes to make fun of people.

    1   2   3   4   5

I laugh to keep from crying.

    1   2   3   4   5

I like to imagine being rich and famous.

    1   2   3   4   5

I like to imagine a better life for myself.

    1   2   3   4   5

I like to just go along with the crowd.

    1   2   3   4   5

I believe that I am responsible for my actions.

    1   2   3   4   5

I believe I can achieve success.

    1   2   3   4   5

I would like to change my attitude.

    1   2   3   4   5

I am anxious for a better life.

    1   2   3   4   5

I am willing to do what is necessary to improve my life.

    1   2   3   4   5

I believe a positive attitude will make a difference in my life.

    1   2   3   4   5

I believe I can get ahead in life if I am given a chance.

    1   2   3   4   5

People seem to want to help me.

     1   2   3   4   5

If somebody does me wrong, I have got to get them back.

     1   2   3   4   5

I want to do things to improve myself.

     1   2   3   4   5

PRACTICAL USES OF THE LEARNING FOR OWNERSHIP PROFILE AND SURVEY IN THE CLASSROOM

The Learning for Ownership Profile can be utilized as a tool to help identify the general characteristics of a specific attitude or behavior. The Learning for Ownership Survey, on the other hand, can be utilized by counselors to assess students and determine whether the concerns identified by teachers on the profile coincide with students' survey responses. The information will help clarify for teachers and counselors how to intervene to help students achieve success.

In my focus group sessions with middle and high school students and public school personnel, the majority of respondents indicated that most students in their schools could be categorized as either profile one (angry) or profile two (apathetic). What they noted in the interviews was interesting. In their experiences at schools with large populations of African American and other ethnic minorities from lower socioeconomic backgrounds, the majority of the students could be categorized as profile one. Some indicated that the anger was largely due to what was going on in their families. The lack of sufficient money to sustain the household is the primary factor causing the distress in some families. Consistently, students indicated that dysfunctional families where parents are divorcing, there is abuse, or there is an absent parent is causing a lot of problems. In one example, the interview highlighted the case of a young teenager who ran away from home to escape the family drama surrounding her parents getting a divorce. The girl was away from home for a week before she was found and taken back home by her dad. In conversation with her, he discovered why she had run away. She said that it was because of her dad and mom. The dad vowed to work through the discord between himself and the mom, and the last report was that the couple was trying to stay together for the children.

Unfortunately, there are also many latchkey children, homeless children, children raising other children, and others who have a host of challenges and issues that confront them that also make them angry. In all instances, it is essential that the mom, dad, or some other family member bond with the child to provide moral support and encouragement. It is clear that the destabilization of families due to the easy divorces and the geographical distances of relatives removes the immediate support system that many children need. With the weakening of the immediate family and the extended family, black children are having fewer refuges to depend upon as a safety net. Consistently, it was indicated in interviews that the young children do not understand why they are angry; they are just responding to their feelings. School administrators in urban school districts indicated that a high percentage of young African American males are being sent to special education because the schools do not know how to handle their anger. It is vital that trained professionals intervene to help students understand the reasons for their feelings and to agree that they, the students, can play an active role in becoming the master of their fate. Interviewees also revealed that the high incidence of profile seven, achievers, could be found in suburban schools where the students were largely from the same middle-class environment, irrespective of the ethnic identification of the students.

So, in effect, the socioeconomic class is identified as the major influencing factor in the stability of students' lives and in the emotions and attitudes that students display. Thus, since the majority of inner-city youth, particularly African American children, are growing up in socioeconomically depressed environments and unstable homes, the traditional model that works for others that lead to success is obviously not working for them, yet students are often treated as though they all have the same view of the world, the same experiences, and the same aspirations.

The survey and profile are helpful tools to determine the attitudes that young people are experiencing. It is important that teachers and counselors work together to provide one-on-one sessions with students about attitudinal matters to help them build their self-esteem. In fact, some of the comments revealed that low self esteem is a major problem that young African American girls are grappling with on a daily basis in public schools today.

Teachers can begin the process to help children restore their lives by reviewing, once again, the early chapters of this book to see what transformative teachers believe and what transformative teachers do. A new job description should be written for school counselors to integrate them more into the case management and support team advocacy work with students. In most interviews, students indicated that they never saw a counselor. Others indicated that they only saw a counselor when it was time to create a schedule. Therefore, it is important that school counselors become more visible and proactive in their work with students.

The Next Steps

The next steps are transformational. They involve taking the Learning for Ownership Empowerment Journey that will result in restructuring students' thoughts, restoring students' lives, and empowering students' futures.

Learning for Ownership Empowerment Model

Learning for Ownership is an empowerment model to enhance African American student success. It involves three components: 1) identifying and classifying students' personal attitudinal profiles; 2) developing and validating students' experiences, thoughts, and beliefs; and (3) creating an ownership culture that links entrepreneurial principles and practices to achievable goals. In the previous chapter, the Learning for Ownership Profile and Survey were presented for practitioners' use to identify and examine students' thoughts, beliefs, experiences, and attitudes. It also provided questions to examine students' receptivity to change. In this chapter, a focus is directed to the second part of the empowerment model: to develop, strengthen, and validate students' experiences, thoughts, and beliefs through a focus on behavioral modification with which trained professional counselors would be involved.

There are two forms of empowerment that can help African American children succeed. The first is the external empowerment that teachers, counselors, family members, and other stakeholders can bestow. The external empowerment is a combination of the kudos, the encouragement, the confidence that others have in an individual that they often display through their comments or through their actions. For example, I have observed that some teachers ask specific students to assist them with various school projects. The teacher's selection of specific students to work on a project or an assignment is a form of empowerment that implies through its actions respect, confidence, and trust. For the student, this act instantly singles him out as a leader and elevates the self-image and the self-esteem.

Internal empowerment, on the other hand, cannot be bestowed by others; it is an empowerment that emanates from within and that the individual must bestow upon himself or work to achieve. The internal empowerment is profoundly gratifying and is achieved through the acquisition of knowledge, skills, abilities, and beliefs that, ultimately, propel students to a heightened level of self-confidence and self-respect. For example, there are students who are extraordinarily disciplined and handle emotionally-charged situations in emotionally-intelligent ways. There are students who are exceptionally skilled in an art or a craft and are empowered by the knowledge that they have acquired. There are other students who have extraordinary speaking, reading, writing, or mathematical abilities and aptitudes; they know it and are supremely self-confident. Then there are others who have an incredible depth of knowledge in specific fields of study and who are empowered by the information they have learned. There are students who are bilingual, well traveled, and conversant about different world cultures. Both types of empowerment, external and internal, are important and can raise students' self-esteem. The more a student empowers himself internally, however, the greater the chances of increasing the self-confidence, self-esteem, and the esteem held by others.

Internal empowerment is life transforming. I am sure you have heard individuals comment on the person who walks around as though he is on top of the world, so to speak. Others look at the person and say, "He is arrogant," or question, "Who does he think he is trying to act important?" There is nothing wrong with that attitude or air, as some refer to it. The person, although potentially penniless, has decided that his view of self is not based upon how much money he has or his personal station in life; his view is based upon the value that he places upon himself. That concept is critically important for young people to understand. The value that they place upon themselves is something that begins with them first and foremost. Therefore, it influences how they talk, dress, and act. It influences the choices they make and the individuals they choose as acquaintances. The questions are, "How much do the students that you know value themselves? Do they value themselves enough to take care of their thoughts, to steer clear of negative people and dangerous situations, to put their best foot forward at all times? There are, no doubt, individuals who, through their behavior, show that they value others more than they value themselves, and they value things more than they value their personal lives. This is the point at which values clarification is essential for young people to help them make moral and ethical choices. A lesson in values clarification could be the turning point that prevents a student from dropping out of school, that raises the consciousness level of students enough to prevent a wrongful act, or to help students shape a life of principles and beliefs that will empower them in their personal and professional lives.

This chapter focuses on three specific areas to develop and validate students' experiences, thoughts, and beliefs. The specific ways to accomplish that goal are to 1) transform the mindset of the students, 2) transform the skill sets of the students, and 3) transform the level of expectations set for the students.

Transform the Mindset

Transforming the mindset is a rather broad, comprehensive topic that involves a number of factors. It requires the students' willingness to change, students' commitment to the change process, and students' open-minded participation in the journey that leads to change. Without their open-mindedness and willingness to engage in the change process, the information—no matter how valuable and life changing—will be equivalent to the expression that says, "What you say goes into one ear and out the other." Obviously, transforming the mindset begins with a personal, vested interest in change. It involves the desire for a better way of life than what they currently have; it involves seeking joyful emotions that they are not currently experiencing, and it involves acquiring material possessions and other assets that they desire. The critical factor is to show students the better way that empowers them internally and externally rather than their resorting to pathways and actions that disempower them. Therefore, practitioners should communicate to students that education is really the better way for them to change their lives, their emotions, and their circumstances. They should also be persuaded that an attitude of expectancy is the proper state of mind. The attitude of expectancy is one that positions the students to look favorably to each day where something positive is likely to happen in their lives as they change their attitudes and emotions and exert the effort required to empower themselves. It is true that once the mindset is fixed, the attitudes, behaviors, and emotions will follow. Therefore, it is important that African American students make up their minds to be a success and not a failure; they will need to decide that they will be victorious and not defeated; they will be the lenders and never the borrowers, and they will be blessed and not cursed anymore.

Basic Nuggets to Sustain Change

Below is what I call basic nuggets or solid gems of information that can help facilitate the change process for African American children, whether used by teachers or counselors.

- Nugget: Help children discover dreams they can pursue. Expose children to the breadth of information that broadens their knowledge and captures their interest for a career pursuit. Teach them how to achieve their dreams and then help connect them with the right information, right people, and right resources to help them achieve their goals. African American children should be persuaded that they cannot achieve maximally until they finally can believe in themselves. Once they truly believe, their actions and their attitudes will reflect their belief. I often use a pledge with public school students whom I talk to that says, "What the mind can conceive and believe, I can achieve." I often have students recite the affirmation with me. Then I ask for a show of hands of those who truly believe that affirmation for themselves. Without failure, over the years, all students have consistently raised their hands in agreement. I wonder, though, how many of the students have actually achieved their goals. For so many of them, they are simply empty vessels wanting to be filled and waiting for someone to help them chart their course, their direction, and their path in life. Where is the conversation being held with African American children about their goals in life? Who is encouraging them and helping them explore options? Where are the role models to help guide them and show them the way? Where are they learning about proper conduct and refining their understanding about social engagement.

There is merit in the popular expression, "Act the part and you can become whatever you want to become." Many people, no matter the race or ethnicity, are taught how to behave in certain situations. There are behaviors that lead to success and those that lead to failure. For example, some of the common behaviors that lead to success are character defining, such as being prompt, honoring deadlines, keeping your word, being a person of integrity, being neat and clean, and exercising the common courtesies.

- Nugget: Prepare students for the prospect that sustained change might require a change in friends and associates from those who think the old way to new friends who think in a way that the student wishes to adopt. A new tier of friends might be the critical factor that elevates students' lives. It could be that the current friends are toxic. Therefore, as a safety net for students, the change process must include a new support system for students and a constant reminder that the student has to live his life in accordance with his clarified values and aspirations; therefore, sacrifices and changes will be necessitated along the journey.

- Nugget: Introduce students to critical-thinking skills to apply in their daily decision-making processes. Students should be reminded that their minds are for constant use in every situation in their lives not only in school but every minute throughout every day – with adults as well as with friends. What process does the student currently use to make decisions? Are the decisions based upon logic, emotion, intuition, or is some other method used? The critical-thinking skills should be taught with a focus on how to process information and how to make decisions. Does the person think for himself, or does he rely upon others to think for him? Does the person make decisions hastily, or does he think through his options? Many students have not considered these questions. Nevertheless, they should understand how, as humans, they are unique and curiously different from all others in creation. Fundamentally, humans are blessed with the ability to think, to reason, and to change their circumstances by making correct and proper choices. While the students know they have a mind and can make choices, they often fail to think because, as I heard one student say, "Thinking is hard work." So, some find it easier to go along with their friends or others who have stronger personalities. This attitude has resulted in negative consequences for too many young people. Practitioners can help students transform their mindset by teaching them how to use their cognitive abilities to arrive at logical conclusions and to help them assess the potential consequences of their choices and their actions. They should be very thoughtful in their analysis in an effort to carefully assess whether their choices will help or harm them.

- Nugget: Illustrate for children that the pathway to transform their lives is through the renewing of their minds with different thoughts, through increasing their exposure to different experiences and opportunities, through enhancing the desire for a better life, and through a confident belief that they can achieve. Ultimately, through exposure and desire, students will develop a belief in themselves that they can achieve. Simply speaking, it seems that changing the mindset should be akin to flipping a switch from "off" to "on" in an effort to change the illumination or lack thereof in a person's life. For many individuals, they are accustomed to living in the dark recesses of their minds or experiencing lack, defeat, or even despair. Therefore, to suggest a different experience for them is a new concept. For those who are simply tired of their dark places in life and who want to make a change, it can be like flipping the switch to "on." Then they can begin to look around themselves and see all of the possibilities before them. In their new journey, they will need facilitators who can guide them and tell them what is available and what to avoid in their illuminated journey and help them travel to their chosen destination, whether a profession, a career, an entrepreneurial venture, or a desired lifestyle.

- Nugget: Provide opportunities for children to dream big dreams that allow them to see beyond their circumstances to envision a better life for themselves. Goal setting is fundamental to allow students to formalize thoughts about their aspirations.

Learning for Ownership challenges young people to think. It challenges them to apply their cognitive skills and abilities. It challenges them to use their minds and apply principles that will empower them to achieve great successes in their lives.

THE ROLE OF STUDENTS

Students play an essential role in activating their personal empowerment to transform their mindset. Practitioners can discuss the commitments with the students and get them to sign a pledge to apply the principles involved in Learning for Ownership for one semester at a time. Following is a list of commitments that are recommended:

- Decide that negative thoughts and beliefs are counterproductive, so students will agree to replace negative thoughts with positive thoughts and beliefs.

- Make a personal decision to commit to a positive, productive life.

- Decide to empower self through the acquisition of knowledge and skills.

- Begin to speak with confidence.

- Apply critical thinking in all decision-making circumstances.

- Learn something new everyday that you can share with family and friends.

- Practice behaviors that you know will make your mother proud.

- Develop socially acceptable ways of communicating verbally and nonverbally.

- Enhance the Learning for Ownership experiences through travels, cultural activities, and other outreach activities.

- Practice presenting the best self through speech, dress, grooming, conversation, and behavior.

- Learn to apply the Golden Rule in your daily life.

- Create a database of role models who serve as a support network.

- Participate in a book club or read socially acceptable literature for at least thirty minutes every day.

- Respond to challenges in emotionally-intelligent ways.

- Serve as a role model for younger African American children.

- Develop goals and a flow chart to success.

Once the mindset is fixed, the attitudes and behaviors will synchronize and follow. Therefore, it is essential as a first step to agree that students desire and commit to change. I have often heard the expression, "You can lead a horse to water, but you cannot make it drink." That is true; and while students are not horses, the analogy is accurate that you cannot force the students to learn. They have to decide that for themselves. Another appropriate expression says, "The attitude determines the altitude." That is often true as well. Practitioners and students working as co-partners in the learning process can facilitate the change in attitudes and the altitude of achievements.

TEACHERS AFFECT THE EXTERNAL EMPOWERMENT

It is a major accomplishment when a person says and means, "I believe in myself and in my abilities." Teachers can help students believe through the external empowerment that they provide. So, for teachers, who are working to change the mindset of students, the following actions are recommended:

- Help students believe in themselves and their ability to succeed.

- Teach to create exposure to options.

- Provide helpful and meaningful resource information to facilitate effective decision making.

- Teach to raise the desire among students to achieve.

- Let students know that you value them every step of the way along their educational journey.

- Create counselor-led student validation groups to listen to students' experiences and to sort through issues associated with their thoughts, beliefs, and experiences.

- Help students set achievable goals.

- Help students to understand the importance of commitment.

- Validate students' successes.

- Teach students how to self validate.

- Help students identify the career pathways that will lead to success for them.

- Help students develop their personal plan for success.

- Show students how to access and use information.

- Help students set the timelines that show benchmarks along the way to goal attainment.

- Help students begin to establish a support network.

- Assign students the responsibility to keep a personal journal that records their Learning for Ownership Empowerment Journey.

- Help students reaffirm their commitment to positive change in their lives.

- Encourage students to participate in a Learning for Ownership network that provides encouragement and support.

TRANSFORM THE SKILL SET

The development of viable skills is empowering both internally and externally. In addition to the self-confidence that is gained, individuals with sought-after skill sets can gain employment opportunities and lucrative incomes. Following are highlights of the skills that employers say are necessary to live and work in a twenty-first century world where knowledge is power. Unfortunately, many African American students have not attained the skills and competencies required for the twenty-first century. Therefore, it is not a surprise that children are not work ready when they graduate from high school; nor is it a surprise that they do not have the skill sets that employers are seeking even for the most basic jobs. It is important for students to at least know what will be expected of them so that, even if the competencies are not embedded in the curricula, proactive students can exercise the initiative to inquire about them and ask their teacher or counselor to help them integrate the skills into their day-to-day activities.

The skill sets that this section highlights are a part of two vital documents. One is the 1991 SCANS (Secretary's Commission on Achieving Necessary Skills) report developed by the United States Department of Labor to identify the specific skills required in the American workplace. And the second is the Twenty-First Century Global Skills. The SCANS are divided into two categories and include the foundational skills and the functional skills. The foundational skills include three major divisions: basic skills, thinking skills, and personal qualities. The basic skills include reading, writing, arithmetic, speaking, and listening. The thinking skills include creative thinking, decision making, problem solving, and knowing how to learn. The personal qualities include responsibility, social skills, self-management, and integrity/honesty. Under the functional skills, there are four major subdivisions that include resources, systems and technology, informational skills, and interpersonal skills. Resources include a focus on how a person manages time, manages money, manages materials/facility resources, and manages human resources. Systems and technology includes the skill set that requires an understanding of systems and the use of technology. The third area of the functional skills is informational skills that includes a focus on how a person acquires and evaluates information, organizes and maintains information, and interprets and communicates information. Interpersonal skills includes a focus on how a person participates as a member of a team, teaches others, serves clients/customers, exercises leadership, and works with cultural diversity. All of the areas are self explanatory.

In grooming African American children for success, the SCANS skills and competencies provide a realistic view of what employers will expect. This tool (SCANS) should be used as the checklist for practitioners. In addition to the SCANS, children should be taught the Twenty-First Century Global Skills that include digital literacy with a focus on global competencies. In the twenty-first century skills, four major overarching areas are addressed, many of which coincide with SCANS. The areas are digital age literacy, inventive thinking, interactive communication, and quality state-of-the-art results. All areas rely heavily upon individuals having the skill sets to use the technology tools and devices to carry out their scope of work.

Transform the Level of Expectations Set for the Students

Perception is reality for many educators. In fact, some educators allow their perception of the populations they are teaching and the stereotypes about the populations influence their behavior and treatment of them. This occurs in many instances where lower expectations are set for African American children than for others. The assumption held by some is that African American children do not want to learn anyway; therefore, anecdotal information, as well as research findings, show that many schools with high percentages of African American children have historically been assigned teachers who are less experienced, less qualified, and more lacking in appropriate credentials to teach in their assigned discipline areas. Many African American children are also directed to special education classes or some other similar program simply because they are not understood or are perceived to be problem-laden kids. In some instances, funding decisions by state agencies and the distribution of dollars to schools suggest that there are double standards for educating children. This double standard translates into lower expectations and lower standards set for inner-city schools which are largely populated by minority students.

The self-fulfilling prophecy is sometimes a factor in students' attainment of knowledge and skills. Therefore, in an effort to raise the level of performance of students, the state and local boards should raise the level of expectations held for African American youth. That increased level of expectation will be communicated verbally and nonverbally to the youth through the goals that are set for the district's schools and the availability of resources and support that the schools receive.

So, how does the empowerment model help develop, strengthen, and validate students' experiences, thoughts, and beliefs? This occurs when the mindset is renewed with healthy, affirming thoughts and beliefs and students have the tools that can be used to accelerate their learning; it occurs when students have acquired competitive skills and competencies that equip them with marketable skills for work in the twenty-first century; and it occurs when governing bodies proclaim the value of educating African American children and demonstrate their support by providing urban, inner-city schools with teachers who have the best and brightest minds and access to the best educational resources to raise the level of education and training that African American children receive. When these areas become the reality, it is at that point that both the internal and external empowerment can catapult students to extraordinary success. A part of the success equation will require students to raise the bar of their own expectations.

Meanwhile, victories are still possible for African American children to experience as they progress step by step along their pathway to a high school diploma by knowing how to clarify their values, how to make quality decisions, and how to take charge of their thoughts and focus their energies in a direction that will empower them and bring success.

Linking Entrepreneurial Principles and Practices to Achievable Goals

One goal of this work is to advance the capability of young African American students to become entrepreneurial in their thinking and in their application of the knowledge and skills they attain. The twenty-first century welcomes great, new ideas, new inventions, and new technologies to promote and to sustain a livable and viable community. Enormous talent is lying dormant while students dismiss many of their educational experiences as being unimportant or insignificant simply because they do not see the value or the relevancy. Statistics reflect the deterioration that is occurring in urban communities and the fallout effects on the lives of many African American children. The students' active participation in a plan to improve their lives is very important and will stretch far beyond themselves and their families to ultimately touch the lives of an entire generation of people in this country and, potentially, around the world. The hope is that the young people will embrace the entrepreneur's vision and incorporate the attributes that are commonly associated with the entrepreneur into their pursuit of education. Those attributes are commonly thought to be self-confidence, passion, intellect, creativity, integrity/honesty, dedication, determination, leadership, commitment, and flexibility. All of the attributes listed are integral to goal attainment, and they provide insight to the competencies needed to be an owner and to learn with the mindset of an owner. This chapter focuses on goal attainment for African American children by linking entrepreneurial principles, practices, and attributes to achievable goals. The subtext of this chapter highlights how self actualization can be achieved through a transformed mindset that students adopt when they view themselves as owners of a growing enterprise called – the self.

Creating an Ownership Culture

Ownership, in this context, refers to the person declaring ownership of himself and everything that pertains to self. Some might say, "This is rather simplistic. The person already has himself." That is true. The person has self physically; but in many instances, the person does not have ownership of self mentally or emotionally. Therefore, ownership of what the person thinks and how he responds to situations is vital and requires education and training. Once an individual masters the ownership of self, he will be able to master the course of his life.

An ownership culture is essential; it is formed by individuals who recognize the privileges of ownership and who want to transmit the value of ownership from one generation to the next. From this vantage point, Learning for Ownership becomes a vital force to transform the lives of African American children by teaching them principles that will guide their success. Reflect on the examples that follow that illustrate how the ownership culture is transmitted.

A young businessman was an invited guest to the home of a very prominent African American entrepreneur. During the visit, he happened to meet the entrepreneur's three sons. All were handsome, well-spoken, intelligent boys between the ages of five and ten years old. Surprisingly, each of the sons had personalized business cards that listed their titles for key positions in the company the dad owned. As the young man was introduced to each child, he received a nice, firm handshake and was presented a business card with the name of the child and the child's future title printed on it. When each son was asked about his future position, each was able to articulate in eloquent details the duties and responsibilities of the position, the company's profile, major competitors in the business, and the key metrics used to monitor their company's success. Needless to say, hearing the story was enormously gratifying. I can only imagine the visitor's surprise at the young boys' maturity.

My husband and I had a similar experience when we attended a social gathering at the home of a prominent African American physician and his wife who is a successful realtor and socialite in the community. As the evening was coming to a close, we began a conversation with the hosts' grandson who was seven years old. When we asked the seven-year-old what he wanted to become when he grows up, he told us in no uncertain terms that he is preparing to become a general surgeon. We responded, "Oh." When we asked the difference between a general surgeon and the type of medicine practiced by his mom, aunt, and grandfather, the young boy also spoke eloquently as he explained the differences.

In the conversation that we had with the young boy, it was apparent that he was well-read and quite comfortable engaging in meaningful conversation. Needless to say, he was quite impressive in his ability to engage in polite conversation and to articulate his opinions. What we noticed throughout the conversation was his use of language to indicate that he is in the preparatory stages of entering his profession.

These are two examples of young African American children who know precisely what their pathways in life will be; and they have claimed ownership in their minds about their personal development and about their direction and purpose in life, so they are inspired and motivated about their present and their future. They are positioned to learn for ownership, and they are already acting the part as an owner. They are performing well in school because they can see the connections between what they are learning and what they aspire to become.

In another conversation, I asked a young boy what he wants to become when he grows up. He said, "I will own my own business. Right now, I am contemplating what that business will be." In conversation with him, he indicated that his dad always tells him to take charge and call the shots. In many instances, when families own businesses, the children learn from observation some of the pleasures and pains associated with ownership. Despite the pains, business owners indicate that they prefer ownership because they determine their future by the decisions they make. This, in a nutshell, is the principle. Ownership requires a mindset that ultimately determines outcomes. Regardless of the type of ownership, education and preparation are required.

For children who do not grow up in homes where their parents are successful business owners, they can still learn the art of ownership success by observing role models who demonstrate the attributes mentioned earlier. No doubt, children who are raised in socioeconomically privileged homes have an advantage in their early exposure. I am persuaded, however, that children who do not have all of the privileges can still attain immeasurable success when they adopt the right mindset and skill sets.

To create an ownership culture for students requires people, time, talent, and resources. There are successful individuals who spend quality time mentoring and nurturing young children. Others donate resources and allow students to shadow them on their jobs. It is clear that the selfless acts such as the College for Kids Programs, are having a positive affect on the development of children.

African American parents, no matter the level of education, skills attainment, or socioeconomic status, can be great advocates for their children. They can provide the encouragement, guidance and support from the home to ensure that the children are attending school and fulfilling the requirements of the school: homework, study time, reading time, and discussion time. In the end analysis, students do not have to languish or depend upon their own limited resources. Schools can become more proactive as well to provide students with the comprehensive learning experiences they need to cope with life in urban areas where crime, poverty, and despair are rampant. The urban ghetto is the environment that so many of the children are eager to flee, sometimes by any means necessary. The way of escape is through their attainment of an education or trade that will lead them to a better quality of life.

Linking Entrepreneurial Principles to Achievable Goals

Entrepreneurial principles discussed in this section are similar to the personal principles that students should set for themselves. In business, the entrepreneur is seeking to meet the demand of society by providing goods and services. His quarterly report provides a balance sheet of profits and losses. For the student, at the early stage of his ownership journey, his balance sheet is his report card that reflects his cumulative gains in academic subject areas. If any area of the report shows less than acceptable performance, that should be a "red flag" for the business owner to direct his special attention. The same is true for students. The students can seek advice from their teachers about how they can improve their performance for the next rating cycle.

In the end analysis, the needs of society will determine the overall success of the business owner and of the student. Both need to be attentive to the market and what it demands. Business owners have to be sensitive to the market and make adjustments if they want to continue their success, and so do students. Students have to decide whether a degree in a field that they like but holds no future employment potential is better than a degree in a field that has long-term demand.

Students like entrepreneurs have to decide on a vision, what ventures they want to pursue, the goals and objectives they want to set, the timelines they will meet, the strategies to attain their goals, and methods to maintain their cash flow, among others. Key to the successes are wise management of time, hard work, and perseverance to attain their goals.

Peter Drucker, author and social ecologist, describes an entrepreneur as someone who actually searches for change, responds to it, and exploits change as an opportunity. Others refer to the entrepreneur as the self-made man. Frederick Douglas, statesman, author, and antislavery abolitionist, was born into slavery in 1818 and is often referred to as a self-made man. Frederick Douglas described what he considers to be the attributes of the self-made man in a speech delivered in 1859. He said, " self-made men are the men who owe little or nothing to birth, relationship, and friendly surroundings; to wealth inherited or to early approved means of education; they are what they are without the aid of any of the favoring conditions by which other men usually rise in the world and achieve great results."

This statement could apply to so many young African American children who can become self-made men and women despite the fact that they have meager beginnings. Despite Frederick

Douglass's circumstances—not knowing his dad, not living with his mom, and being passed from one household to another—he was able to rise above his circumstances, acquire an education, and become a person of great prominence. Despite the circumstances of students today, the same success is possible if they according to Douglass, "work, work, work."

The first big agenda item is to help students develop a vision and a goal. The goals can start as big ideas, but they should be narrowed to include the incremental steps or milestones to goal attainment. The goals are critically important because the student is really investing in himself. The process is really a joint venture between the student and the school, with taxpayers being the financier. In this venture, students are really the start-up enterprise. Most start-ups fail because they do not have a business plan, they are not connected to those who can properly advise and guide them through the process, they do not manage their time and resources well, and they do not attend to the details of their business. At the end of the day, the business flounders due to the lack of a clear vision and the lack of attention to planning in an effort to ensure the business's success. Students who are learning for ownership can rectify these pitfalls that currently affect so many students today who do not manage their time wisely, who do not attend classes, who do not complete assignments, who fail to prepare and, eventually, they drop out. The financier and/or society could say there is no room for dropping out when education is being underwritten as an investment to fulfill the overall current and future needs of society. The expectation is that every investment will bring a high rate of return; and through the ownership culture, it will.

Students essentially have twelve years, in many instances, at taxpayers' expense, for their enterprise to succeed or fail. It is up to the students in consultation with their team of advisors (parents, teachers, counselors, recruiters) to decide how they will take advantage of that advance, up-front support. As you know, business ventures are established primarily to make a profit and secondarily to create and serve a need. The primary principle of business is simple: Is there a demand whereby this business can sustain itself and be profitable? Every student should view his learning as an ownership venture because it really is. The students are partners with society, with society investing in them as chief executive officer of an enterprise that cultivates who and what they will become in life. A smart CEO will learn the principles of good business management and apply the principles to himself. The company is the person named, and the employees at this time include teachers, the school district's administration and staff. The investment amount is the cost of schooling, housing, clothing, all underwritten by either the parents or the taxpayers. At the end of each quarter reporting cycle, students should be able to show a gain in their learning and in their skills as they progress toward their goals. This should be reflected in the demonstrated knowledge, skills, and competencies that students have acquired during that cycle.

Society has a right to expect a return on investment for the dollars spent on public education. It is clear that society has demands for employees in many career pathways. In fact, the demand outstrips the supply of available trained persons to fill the void. As new and emerging businesses start, the demand for talent will continue to increase and the skill sets will become more specialized. Where is the talent pool to replace retirees, to fill new jobs, to fill current jobs? And who will have the competencies to become the next generation of entrepreneurs? The answer resides in the students who learn for ownership.

HELPING STUDENTS SET ACHIEVABLE GOALS

It is time that everyone in the education pipeline becomes more accountable: students, parents, teachers, administrators, school boards, and all persons who consider themselves stakeholders in the future of an educated society. Everyone can play a vital and active role. It is recommended that students, first and foremost, learn how to write and set achievable and measurable goals. The goals should be linked to a profession or a career that the students want to pursue. Some schools prepare students to set career goals by hosting career-day events. These events usually involve professionals from various career fields coming to campus to talk to students about entry-level pathways to their career or profession. The guests answer questions about what the careers entail, how long it will take to complete their training to enter the careers, and the earning potential. For example, if a student wants to become a chemist, career advisors can discuss the pathways and answer all questions about the field. If the student is interested in nursing or allied health, representatives can respond similarly.

When students begin their career planning, they should have a Learning for Ownership Portfolio that allows them to keep a record of their goals, learning objectives, outcomes, references, and experiences that employers will want to review. Some of the standard questions that students should address in their personal Learning for Ownership Portfolios are the following:

- What is my career goal?
- What are the specializations that are included in my career goal?
- Which of the specializations am I particularly interested in working toward?
- What support systems will I need as I work toward my career goal?
- What are the likely obstacles that I must prepare to overcome as I pursue my goal?
- What type of training or education is required?

- What financial aid support is available?

- What is my timeline to complete my program of study?

- Where do I want to be in five years, ten years, and fifteen years?

- Do I want to work for someone else, or do I want to start my own business?

- What lifestyle decisions will I have to make until I achieve my goal?

- What are the names and company profiles of three major companies that employ individuals in my chosen field? Where are the companies located?

- Will I be willing to relocate to accept a job in my career field?

- What steps do I need to take to complete my goal? (Start with the current grade level.)

- What experiences will I have along the way that can be incorporated into my job resume?

Visions and aspirations broaden with exposure and experience. As students' knowledge expand and their associations broaden, it is very likely that they will change their minds about their aspirations. That is fine if those aspirations evolve. The intent is to get students started with an initial plan that can be modified and refined until they finally decide where their career passion really lies for a lifetime commitment.

COMBINING THE TYPOLOGY AND EMPOWERMENT MODEL FOR SUCCESS

In order for Learning for Ownership to have a transforming effect, students who are grappling with issues caused by negative race identification, sociocultural issues, and low self esteem must be willing to identify the source of the problems and then decide to overcome them and move forward. They cannot move forward as long as they remain in their self-pity and anger. Teachers can assist students by referring them to counselors to help them sort through their problems. In the end analysis, students will need to make a quality decision to either retain the self-defeating attitudes and emotions they have or to change their mindsets and leave their past behind so they can work toward a better life.

Students who have a profile in categories one through five can benefit from a discussion about the empowerment model and how to change their lives. They must understand that their disposition is slowly leading to their individual demise by wasting a precious opportunity to maximize their learning and their education at society's expense in all fifty states of the United States. Students who are in stages six and seven can benefit from their internal empowerment to sustain a proper mindset, to continue to expand their skill sets, and to maintain a high level of expectations for themselves. Family members who have a vested interest in their children's success are encouraged to become active participants in ensuring that their children succeed. Many parents have been silent. In part, their silence is due to their own tattered lives and their tangled web of personal issues. Once they understand the insidious cycle that develops, they should become proactive to ensure that their children do not succumb to a hopeless, defeated life. Following are concise recommendations for each of the stages of the typology to help students and practitioners. The primary instruction in all categories is to transform the mindset, transform the skill set, and raise the level of expectations. If the mindset is already fully transformed, then the student should continuously focus on transforming the skill set and continuously raising the level of expectations.

Profile One: The Angry Student

It is recommended that the angry students understand that they can remain in their anger and suffer a worsening condition in their lives, or they can make a quality decision to change. Everyone has issues. Once they understand the source or their anger, they should be given the opportunity to channel their energy into a positive direction to change the course of their lives. As they seek to exercise their options, the students can decide to remain angry and allow those emotions, along with the consequences of their actions to destroy them, or they can decide to change. The decision must be theirs. If they choose to maintain anger, that anger should be directed at their past with a vow that it will not destroy their present and their future.

Profile Two: The Apathetic Student

Apathy is akin to a slow death. Apathetic students run the risk of becoming faceless, nameless individuals. Once again, the students should understand the source of their apathy and recognize that there are no sympathizers with apathetic individuals. Their lives are intended for purpose. If they would like to discover their purpose, then every effort should be made to change their attitudes and to become a participant in shaping their lives.

Profile Three: The Skeptic

The skeptic has potential and has chosen to question all things. There is nothing wrong with inquisitiveness as long as there is forward movement in a direction that is positive and constructive. The skeptic should pursue his academics and a career field that allows him to make full use of his skepticism.

Profile Four: The Player

The player, on the other hand, should become more serious about his work. He is quick witted and has a bright mind, but he needs to be focused, and his energy should be harnessed to participate in productive efforts. Changing the mindset of the player should be an easy process, for he is starving for someone to genuinely show concern for him. The player's career inventory will reflect careers that will allow him to utilize his social skills and his ability to entertain others. This will help connect the player's natural personality and leaning to a career goal that can lead to a productive life.

Profile Five: The Dreamer

The dreamer has great ideas and is bright. His career aspirations are likely to change every six months because there is so much that interests him. He has not had the privilege of writing goals and targeting a specific career that he would like to pursue. The dreamer is sometimes a dabbler and could benefit from a career inventory that would highlight the best career matches for him. With proper guidance, focus, and perseverance, the dreamer can move forward to the attainment of his goal.

Profile Six: The Realist

The realist needs guidance and support to further affirm what he has already figured out: that education is essential. The realist knows what is possible for him but can be stretched beyond his comfort level to achieve even greater successes. The primary need of the realist is the external support to achieve his goals. The realist will sometimes make choices that will limit his level of attainment because of the level of responsibility to others that he feels.

Success does not happen by accident. The Achiever knows this and works hard to achieve. The achiever is afraid of failure and works hard to excel in every area. The achiever is adept at finding solutions to problems that occur and in overcoming obstacles in order to accomplish his goals.

CONCLUSION

In all instances, students must decide what will be their value to themselves, and what will be their value to society. Society is in need of more persons who claim ownership, those who are entrepreneurs, and those who are self-made men and women who can, through taking ownership of their lives, accomplish great goals.

Practitioner Application of the Empowerment Model

One of the questions that this chapter answers for teachers is how to operationalize the information and principles presented to transform the mindset, the skill set, and level of expectation of students. Strategies for practical application will be presented.

As one strategy, teachers can use the Learning for Ownership Empowerment Model as a template to plan and organize their lessons. While this tool is not intended to replace the lesson plan template that is recommended by the school district, components of the empowerment model can, nonetheless, be incorporated into the template that teachers currently use. The empowerment model focuses on transforming the mindset of students, transforming the skill sets of students, and raising the levels of expectations of and for students. As in any lesson-planning process, the teacher should prepare with the intended outcomes in mind. In this case, it includes the following questions: How will the lesson help transform the mindsets of students? How will the lesson help transform the skill sets of students? How will the lesson challenge students and help to raise their levels of expectations?

Following is a checklist with brief explanatory notes that practitioners can use when preparing lessons to guide their inclusion of the empowerment principles. First is a checklist to keep in mind when working on lessons to transform the mindset.

Transform the Mindset

Teachers should consider the following questions and write responses to them when developing the lesson plan. This approach is an effective process to ensure that the lesson incorporates opportunities to improve students' knowledge, skills, and behaviors. Also, when students know what is expected of them in the learning process, they are apt to retain information much better and the outcomes are apt to be improved. It is an aid to effective instruction and the impartation of knowledge, skills, and behaviors when students know precisely what is expected of them. The questions that teachers should be able to address that relate to transforming the mindset follow.

- What is the purpose of the lesson?

- What are the core objectives of the lesson that I want students to learn?

- What are the learning experiences that students will engage in to help meet the course objectives?

- What should students know and be able to do upon completion of the lesson?

- What specific ways should the lesson impact the attitudes and behaviors of students?

- What are the outcome measures or key performance indicators that will be utilized to measure student success?

- How is the lesson relevant to students' lives: school life; home life; social life, and life with family, friends, and acquaintances?

- What is the knowledge and content that students will derive from this lesson?

- What critical thinking skills will students learn from the lesson that they can apply in their daily lives?

- How does this lesson help students identify values that individuals and groups hold?

- What are the students' personal opinions about the values expressed in the lesson?

- What types of tests will be administered to assess student learning?

The second area of the empowerment model focuses on transforming the skill set. Transforming the skill set allows students to demonstrate their attainment of the necessary skills and the application of skills in their lives. Transforming the skill set focuses on the applied approach to learning wherein students learn by doing. The checklist for the second component of the empowerment model includes the following questions that teachers should answer in preparing their lesson plans.

Transform the Skill Set

- What skills should students be able to demonstrate after completing the lesson?

- How can students apply the learned skills in their daily lives?

- How will competency in demonstrating the skills be measured?

- In what situations can students demonstrate the learned skills?

- How does the lesson help to improve students' ability to interact effectively with diverse cultural, ethnic, and international groups?

- What key terms should students understand, define, and be able to use in sentences upon completion of the lesson?

The third area focuses on transforming the level of expectations of and for students. This area concentrates on the expectations that others set for students, and it includes the level of expectations that students set for themselves. For example, perceptions and stereotypes that others have might often influence what they expect. Therefore, if the perception of the students' ability is low, then the level of expectation might also be low. If, on the other hand, there is the perception that the students are advanced and capable, then the expectations might also rise to that high level. What I have discovered in my years of teaching, however, is that students usually rise to the level of expectations set for them. That is why the intent of Learning for Ownership is to develop the whole student.

Transform the Level of Expectations

Teachers are limited in what they can do to raise the levels of expectations outside of their sphere of immediate influence. Many of the factors that impact quality teaching reside under the authority of others, like principals, superintendents, board members, state legislators, and other stakeholders who make higher-level decisions pertaining to administrative matters, policy decisions, and funding. Nevertheless, there are areas that teachers can control, such as their individual classrooms. Teachers can become the silver bullet that, despite the circumstances, helps transform the thinking of students and put them on the pathway to success. I have heard countless examples from students about their teachers, irrespective of the race or ethnicity, who literally changed their lives. The one point that resonated with each of them was the teacher's high expectations of them. I recommend that in the lesson planning, that teachers address the following areas to transform the level of expectations: a focus on student success, a focus on students' attainment of knowledge and skills, a focus on pedagogy, a focus on the classroom environment, a focus on technology, a focus on classroom resources, and a focus on the use of multimedia. Each of the areas is briefly discussed below.

A Focus on Student Success

A Learning for Ownership Student Success Plan should be developed for each student in every class that reminds him that success is the only option. The Learning for Ownership Plan should include the purpose and objectives of the course and of each lesson and how the content applies to students' everyday lives. In addition to the purpose, goals, and objectives of the course, it involves a list of recommended readings and learning outcomes for the semester. Students should be able to manage their Learning for Ownership Plan by including copies of their graded work, homework, tests, and any written reflections they might have undertaken as they participated in their Learning for Ownership journey. On a weekly basis, students should review and reflect upon their past performance and make notes on how they can improve.

A Focus on the Attainment of Knowledge and Skills

The time spent in class should be used constructively for teachers to teach and for students to learn. There should not be a day off or down time when it comes to the business of teaching and learning. Every minute spent should count. Diversifying the learning experience is important. Thus, teachers can create learning experiences that allow students to show demonstrated mastery of the subject being taken even prior to test time. Students can participate in group sessions and other learning experiences to master the goals that are set. Teachers should focus on the content of the subject matter to ensure that students acquire the essential knowledge and understand how to apply it. They should focus on the skills so students will know how to demonstrate and apply the skills they have acquired, and they should focus on the application of the learning to students' lives.

A Focus on the Pedagogy

In developing the pedagogy, first and foremost, teachers should consider the subject matter to be taught, the learning styles of students who are enrolled in the class, and the best way to make the connection instructionally with the students so they can learn and apply the information being studied. Some instructors teach to the middle fifty percent of the class. This approach is a disservice to students who are grouped in the bottom and top rankings of the class. Neither group outside the middle is being equipped to perform at its best. In classes where students are at different performance levels, individualized instruction along with learning communities is recommended.

A Focus on the Classroom Environment

The teacher has control over the configuration of the classroom for various learning experiences. There are occasions when chairs should be positioned for a lecture format or in small circles for learning communities or for other small group-collaborative work sessions. Teachers also create the ambience of the classroom through the creativity exercised to display positive and supportive messages, whether on a blackboard, a whiteboard, or a bulletin board, to encourage and support student success. As a former student, I am sure you recall teachers whose classrooms you looked forward to attending because of the special efforts the teacher made to create a student-friendly and engaging environment for learning to occur. By the same token, I am sure you can also think of those classrooms that you dreaded going to because the environment was not student-friendly, the classroom was not properly equipped, and the teacher was not properly prepared to teach the course. Those were the teachers who would ask the class, "What do you want to do today?"

A Focus on Technology

Technology as a teaching tool is essential in today's twenty-first century learning environment. The technology should be available, functional, and portable. Ideally, all students should have access to a laptop computer or some other smart technology device to allow for access to the Internet and the other vast range of teaching and learning tools available. Without question, all teachers and students should be computer literate. Teachers, irrespective of the discipline, can integrate computer skills into the lesson no matter the subject being taught.

A Focus on Resources

Up-to-date appropriate teaching tools, such as microscopes, textbooks, technology, software, and other materials should be made available for students to use in the classroom. Teachers can advocate for the latest technology and teaching tools to be used based upon curricular needs. I have heard horrendous examples of urban schools where sufficient numbers of computers were not available for instruction in computer technology, so students did not have the applied, hands-on experience. Instead, they watched their instructor demonstrate use of the computer through illustrations projected onto the classroom wall.

A Focus on the Use of Multimedia

Teachers can assess their students to identify how they learn best, whether via cooperative or collaborative learning or via some other style. It is recommended that diverse modalities be utilized to enhance student learning particularly for boys and girls, since according to brain-based research, boys and girls learn differently. The traditional lecture format can be enhanced by the use of multimedia in classroom instruction. The use of video, teleconferencing, and audio conferencing can enrich student learning by connecting students with their peers in their city, their state, the nation, or the global community to discuss pertinent issues and to broaden the connections with others in various parts of the world.

The primary impetus is to achieve two desired ends. The first is to improve the learning experiences for students, and the second is for students to achieve the desired educational outcomes. It is recommended that the subject matter be delivered in compelling ways that are certain to capture and maintain the interest of the students. This can be accomplished in many ways: through lecture, multimedia, collaborative group work, independent study, and other teaching strategies. Research shows that for African American students, the cooperative learning strategy is quite effective. The intent of multiple teaching strategies is to maximize the students' learning experience and to prepare them for the real world where team work, collaboration, and flexibility are required. To improve the learning experience for all students, it is important for teachers to adopt the beliefs and actions of transformative teachers.

The Role of Students

Students who are committed to the principles involved in Learning for Ownership must do the following:

- Take ownership responsibility for what they are to learn in their classes.

- Consider their time at school as their time on the job where work is expected of them.

- Write down notes in class and review the notes at the end of the day. If there are questions about what is in the notes, ask the teacher during the next class period. Rewrite the notes for clarity so they are complete and accurate when preparing for a test.

- Read the assignments and make notes about the reading.

- Write down questions that arise from the homework and ask the teacher for clarification.

- Work with the teacher to maintain a personalized Learning for Ownership Plan for each course.

In the end analysis, the learning experience belongs to each student. The best approach to the experience is to embrace it and to get maximum benefit from it every day.

Student Engagement

Student engagement is also critically important to ensure that students are involved in activities that will motivate them to persist in school to complete their course, their grade, and their diploma. There are many ways to involve students to ensure that they persist in school and achieve mandated competencies at high rates of performance. Some students, for example, are engaged through the clubs, organizations, and activities such as organized team sports. Other students are engaged in internship experiences to gain job experiences and advanced familiarity with a career field that they might be interested in pursuing; others are involved in service learning where they participate as a volunteer with a company, small business, or civic association to work on a specific project. Finally, some students are involved in civic engagement where they work on projects, sometimes sponsored by the school in partnership with a community organization to raise awareness about a specific activity, such as recycling, global warming, and other issues that address civic matters. In all instances, the learning experience is enriched due to the skills students learn from collaborative group work on matters of civic importance. The skills far exceed those that would be gained by reading about civic engagement or participating in civic engagement exercises in the classroom. Instead, students get the opportunity to work alongside community persons and learn about the history of neighborhoods and the economics and politics of decision making.

Use of the Empowerment Model to Teach Twenty-First Century Global Skills

There is so much for students to know and learn that no day should be void of new information. Many students, as evidenced by statistics, are not academically prepared to compete in the twenty-first century, neither locally, nationally, nor internationally. It is no longer the neighbor next door or the student in the next state who creates the competition for students in the United States; it is the student in another, remote part of the world.

Many African American students as a group, by and large, have so much to learn to be competitive nationally; nevertheless, students can gain great strides and improve exponentially if there is a will both in the student and in the schools. It requires each person to hold every other person accountable to make the educational investment substantial and meritorious. It also requires each teacher, each school administrator, and each state's legislature to recognize that their threat does not reside in the provision of quality education to African American children, nor is the threat a factor of race or ethnicity. The potential threat to our nation resides in the failure to educate sufficient numbers of scientists, skilled technicians, deep thinkers, statesmen, and people in all essential professions and fields to occupy all of the essential roles required by society.

Finally, the twenty-first century experience is being lived in the context of a heterogeneous global society. These are not the good old days of the early years of the twentieth century when the three *R*'s were the standard for education. Today, multiple literacies are required to live, work, and have a desirable quality of life in this, a twenty-first century global society. It is essential for African American students to learn effective communication skills to interact with others. The international borders have blurred, and nations are able to communicate more easily than ever before, all due to the availability and speed of the Internet. This open channel to the world creates a new dynamic that involves people from different cultural groups, language groups, racial groups, and religions to have contact with one another and, at some point, interact with one another.

Global understanding of diverse groups can be facilitated by the teacher incorporating information about the following into lesson planning: a knowledge of the history and culture of nations; a knowledge of the cultural traditions, values, and symbols of various cultures; historical relations of other nations with the United States of America; familiarity with the spoken language of diverse groups; and demographic information about educational attainment, economics, politics, the role of the family, and the role of males and females in other cultures of the world.

As teachers prepare their lessons, careful thought should be given to the readings or other assignments to highlight the multicultural richness of the country and of the world. Students who function best in the global society will be those who have the knowledge and the skill sets to add value to society in a productive way and who can communicate effectively with others.

Now, having detailed all of this information, I know there are some teachers who will take the information and use it to enhance instruction. Then, there are others who will dismiss the information and continue with the attitude "I've got my education. These children will need to get theirs." As a teacher, there are high expectations placed upon them by society to be the gatekeepers to the next generation of professionals. As the gatekeepers, teachers are expected to demonstrate the highest level of professional ethics to ensure that all students are treated equally and taught with the highest levels of intellect, skillfulness, accuracy, and precision. The ability to touch the hearts and minds of present and future generations is what makes teachers a special breed. The future that unfolds will be a reflection of the effectiveness at which the teachers of the nation performed their jobs and made a significant difference.

Part Three

Part three focuses entirely on what happens to African American children after they have been introduced to their Learning for Ownership Journey. Practitioners are provided the metrics that can be used to evaluate student performance and achievement. Additionally, educational stakeholders are provided a proposed plan of action to reengineer failing urban schools in a way that will benefit the students, the schools, the workforce, and the larger society.

Empowered for Success
in a Twenty-First Century
Global Society

One purpose of this book is to raise the consciousness levels of educational practitioners and to equip them with information that will build their confidence when they are teaching African American children. The practitioners are the key facilitators who can start the children on a magnificent journey to learn for ownership and achieve abundant success in life. Can you imagine the gravitas of society with more individuals educated and prepared to make meaningful contributions? That is the future that we all aim for as we strive each day to become better and to contribute more. This is the time and the place for everyone to coalesce and to make a difference. We know from the research data that many African American children are grappling with many issues: negative race identification, negative perceptual and sociocultural issues, and others; but comparatively speaking, all people, irrespective of their race, ethnicity, or gender, have grappled with issues in life, some which will be discussed later in this chapter as examples of how people can rise above their circumstances to achieve greatness.

Let us reflect for a moment on a point in history where, despite the challenges, former slaves who were faced with the choice of life as they once knew it on the slave plantation or life as freedmen opted for the latter. In 1863, with the abolition of slavery, Booker T. Washington, in his book, *Up From Slavery*, recounts the joy that slaves experienced when they received the news of their freedom followed by the despair they felt when they realized they had no home other than the former slave quarters, no skills other than the house or field work they had done for the slave master, and no way to provide for themselves and for their families other than the handouts and generosity of the former slave owners. The Emancipation Proclamation came quickly, and the masses had not prepared themselves to live as free men and women. Nevertheless, some former slaves still launched out to create a new life for themselves. Those who launched out were fearless, courageous, and daring, realizing that the life they could create for themselves would be better than what they had, so they were willing to make the sacrifice and to take a chance on a better way. The better way for them was to take control of their lives. For others, they chose the familiar and returned to the plantation. Many former slaves such as the ones mentioned in this book, however, had an unquenchable thirst for knowledge and learning. They empowered themselves with education to establish a better life for themselves and for their children. Given the tenacity and the determination of so many freed slaves to acquire an education juxtaposed with the state of African American children today, I can only imagine the spirits of the abolitionists crying out for the children and children's children to rise up and cloak themselves with self-reliance and self-sufficiency at which the world will marvel and appreciate. Of course, it is important to understand one's history and learn from it, but it is not acceptable to allow history and a tradition of servitude to limit dreams, aspirations, and drive to rise above circumstances to achieve a better life.

To be successful in the twenty-first century requires a personal commitment from each person that each will do better and do more within his or her scope to educate, to train, to learn, and to mentor the next generation. This also means that students today must accept the responsibility to serve as role models and mentors for their siblings or others who are watching them and patterning their behaviors and their choices after them. I am persuaded that education continues to be the key to opportunity and to a better life; we simply need more willing, active participants.

Igniting the Educational Revolution

Learning for Ownership, is the capstone of dual credit. It is the raison detre to justify why students should engage in educational pursuits at all. The Learning for Ownership mindset must begin with students when they are first able to speak and comprehend. They must be taught with the mantras that they have to believe in themselves, and they have to know that they can achieve. They must be taught to treat others as they wish to be treated. They must be trained to be resilient and to never give up on their dreams. They must have a *why*, as described by Dr. Victor Frankyl in his book, Man's Search for Meaning, to sustain them during the challenging times of their lives.

Dr. Victor Frankyl discusses the self-transcendence that leads to true meaning that individuals gain from life. There are three ways that we, according to Dr. Frankyl, gain the self transcendence: 1) doing a noble work or doing a deed, 2) by experiencing a value, such as the beauty of art that influences a person's work with others, and 3) through suffering (Frankyl, 176). When an individual experiences suffering, that suffering typically propels him to a service for a higher good.

In this new era, a self-transcendence is needed in education. It should be coupled with the empowerment of educational practitioners who can help turn the dial to create purpose in African American children's lives. That compelling force to help others discover their purpose can emanate from the practitioner's encouragement of students to 1) meet the need of another person, 2) to create change or to right a wrong that the student feels has occurred, and 3) to impact generations for a greater cause. Each of the areas will be discussed with examples that illustrate how teachers and other professionals encouraged their students and helped them to discover their purpose.

EMPOWERED TO MEET A NEED

Throughout this work, the need has been demonstrated for well-prepared students, for dedicated teachers, and a team of advocates for student success. Individuals have to personally feel the need before they can fully devote themselves to a cause that is greater than themselves. That cause can be translated into the future of their children, grandchildren, or even their great grandchildren. Or it can be translated into their desire to preserve our beloved country and its values. Finally, it can be translated into the personal desire to ensure that they are well cared for in their old age years by people who have the knowledge, training, and skills to attend to them as physicians, nurses, dieticians, and professionals in other critical areas.

What is it that causes individuals to see a cause greater than themselves and to embrace it? In many instances, they have no physical or financial interest invested in the cause, but it is a cause that they truly believe in and to which they want to fully devote themselves. Where does the motivation emanate from that causes an individual to sell his home and all of his worldly possessions and to leave his family to pursue a cause? These are the types of individuals that the twenty-first century needs to ensure that the vision of a more perfect union is realized for all of the people.

There are so many diverse ways that people can pick up the mantle and help create a more perfect union of educated African American students. The onus is not singularly on the teachers, although teachers spend the better part of the school day with the children and help shape their values. The commitment is one that must be felt and shared by all. As Booker T. Washington said in his Atlanta Exposition Address on September 18, 1895, "The laws of changeless justice bind, oppressor with the oppressed, and close as sin and suffering joined—we march to fate abreast." And so it is with the educated and the uneducated, the rich and the poor, the adults and the children, the majority and the minority that we all march to fate abreast.

There is truth in the statement made by Mahatma Gandhi, "We have to be the change that we want to see in society." So what is the change that you want to see? Do you want to see a more wholesome society with better communities, less dependency upon social services, more educated persons, lower unemployment, an end to the cycle of poverty? Do you want to see a robust talent pool of individuals who have exceptional credentials to fill the jobs that are currently unfilled? What do you want to see? If what you want to see is for the betterment of society, what do you plan to do about it now? Sometimes, to initiate change, the people facilitating the change have to radically change their perspectives and decide that when they help someone else, they are also indirectly helping themselves.

Think about individuals who rose from the ranks of obscurity to become great successes simply because there was a need and the person who became famous in meeting that need did not, on the surface, appear to be the one who could meet the need. Let us reflect on a great and notable scientist such as Sir Isaac Newton who was born in England in January 1643. At an early age, he was not considered the most likely to succeed primarily because his life circumstances, and his behavior did not fit the norm of the status quo. But his teacher recognized his potential and provided him encouragement and support. One can only imagine the void that would have remained even today if the teacher had not been a major influencing factor in Sir Isaac Newton's life.

Isaac Newton was raised in a single-parent home. His dad had died before Isaac was born. His mother eventually remarried a man of very modest means; however, as a part of the marriage arrangement, Isaac could not live with his mother and stepdad. He lived with his grandmother, who raised him. Isaac is said to have been terribly inattentive in school. Once he acquired a job, he is also said to have skipped work on more than one occasion and was found sitting under a shade tree. It was allegedly one of the times when he was sitting under a tree that he saw an apple fall to the ground. It was that single act that spurred his concept of the law of gravity. Isaac was skilled with his hands and spent his time making sun dials, model windmills, and such, and one of his former teachers who recognized his intellectual gifts encouraged his mother to allow him to prepare for entrance to the university. After he was admitted, because of his financial hardship, he lived at the home of a business leader, a pharmacist, and had to work performing various menial domestic services. He graduated from Cambridge University and became a physicist, mathematician, natural philosopher, and is still today considered one of the most important scientists of all time, formulating laws of universal gravitation and motion, laws that explain how objects move on Earth as well as through the heavens. He established the modern study of optics, built the first reflecting telescope, and is the inventor of the area of mathematics called calculus. Sir Isaac Newton's comment about his success was as follows: "If I can see farther than others, it is only because I stand on the shoulders of giants." Despite the fact that some claimed that he had neurosis and insecurity caused by the early abandonment that affected him, he, nonetheless, made major contributions to society. How are your students' lives so different from Sir Isaac Newton's in the early beginnings? Sir Isaac Newton could have resorted to anger, apathy, a dependency complex, or some other counterproductive disposition, but instead chose to become an achiever and make significant contributions that the world will always remember. Similarly, I believe in the transcendence and the empowerment of students who embrace the reins to their future. With the support of teachers, counselors, principals, and others, they too, like Sir Isaac Newton, will be able to say they can see farther because of the shoulders of giants that they stand upon.

The same type of human drive to meet a need was evident in Dr. Charles R. Drew. He lived a short life, but he also met a significant need to which the world is grateful. Dr. Charles R. Drew was born in June 1904 in Washington, DC. Dr. Drew was a medical doctor and surgeon who started the blood bank idea leading to a system for the long-term preservation of blood plasma. He was from modest beginnings. His dad laid carpet for a living, and his mom was a teacher who quit her job after Charles Drew's birth to raise him. His parents were poor but stressed the importance of education. His dad allegedly told his children, "Do what you believe in. Take a stand and don't get licked." In effect, his dad was telling him, "Do not give up on what you believe in."

George Washington Carver was born in 1864, one year after the Emancipation Proclamation. He was determined to acquire an education. In fact, a statement made about him indicates the following: "A single urge of learning has overcome the sufferings and hardships of slave life." George Washington Carver, like so many others, experienced the degradation of prejudice and discrimination, but he was destined to meet a need. He is noted in history as "one of the greatest examples of dedication in human history. Everything that he invented, he invented for the benefit of mankind." George Washington Carver promoted alternatives to cotton so farmers, many of whom were poor, would have a source of their own food and other products. George Washington Carver created approximately a hundred products from the peanuts and 105 food recipes that used peanuts. A lady by the name of Mariah Watkins, a person from whom he rented a room to attend school, told him, "You must learn all you can and then go back out into the world and give your learning back to the people." Despite all of his hardships and struggles, George Washington Carver persisted toward his goal and graduated from Iowa State University with a master's degree in 1896, prior to going to Tuskegee Institute, where he spent the remainder of his career.

Empowered to Create Change or to Make Right a Wrong

Some people believe that they are living at the time that they are alive for a specific reason. They have the talent and the abilities to do things that others are unable to do. They forge ahead despite the apparent obstacles and achieve greatness. Take as an example former US Supreme Court Justice Thurgood Marshall, who, when appointed to the United States Supreme Court by former President Lyndon B. Johnson in 1967, President Johnson said the following about him: "This is the right thing to do, the right time to do it, the right man and the right place."

That statement is quite profound. As you examine Supreme Court Justice Marshall's ascendancy to the high court, it is interesting to note that all of the positions that he held and the barriers that he experienced were preparatory stepping stones to his eventual high office. Thurgood Marshall was born in Baltimore, Maryland, on July 2, 1908. He was the great grandson of a slave. He experienced outright discrimination during his life, and particularly when he wanted to apply to law school at the University Of Maryland School of Law but was told by the Dean of the University that he would not be accepted because of the school's segregation policy. Being determined, Thurgood Marshall attended Howard University's School of Law instead. He received his law degree in 1933 at the age of twenty-five and graduated first in his class. Ironically, as an attorney, he successfully represented a client in a suit against the University of Maryland School of Law for its segregation policy in the Murray vs. Pearson Case. Marshall was successful in many other cases as well, even after he became the chief counsel for the National Association for the Advancement of Colored People (NAACP). He argued successfully before the US Supreme Court on many cases, including Brown vs. the Board of Education of Topeka in 1954, which resulted in the call for desegregation of public schools "with all deliberate speed."

Despite the barriers, the discrimination, and the prejudicial climate at the time, Thurgood Marshall, like so many other African American men and women of purpose, had the burning desire to fulfill the calling on his life. As former President Johnson said, "This is the right thing to do, the right time to do it, the right man and the right place."

What would have happened to Marshall if he had acquiesced or become angry? What if he had given up on his future because of circumstances? As many have said over the years, circumstances change. They certainly did for Supreme Court Justice Marshall. Thurgood Marshall was appointed to the highest court in the land 104 years after the Emancipation Proclamation.

One of the persons to help Marshall fulfill his purpose was the President of the United States of America.

Empowered to Impact Generations
for a Greater Cause

As an example of one who made an impact on generations for a greater cause is Mary Jane McLeod Bethune who was born on July 10, 1875, and started a school for African American students in Daytona Beach, Florida, named Bethune-Cookman University. In addition to starting a school for African Americans, Mary Jane McLeod Bethune was also an advisor to President Franklin D. Roosevelt. Mary McLeod Bethune was born in South Carolina to parents who had been slaves. She was the fifteenth of seventeen children and began working in the fields at age five. She knew the struggles of the time and the hardships to gain equality, yet she learned how to create alliances and to make a mark for future generations. As a part of her last will and testament, she says:

> I leave you love. I leave you hope. I leave you the challenge of developing confidence in one another. I leave you a thirst for education. I leave you a respect for the use of power. I leave you faith. I leave you racial dignity. I leave you a desire to live harmoniously with your fellow men. I leave you, finally, a responsibility to our young people.

The responsibility that Mary McLeod Bethune referenced in her last will and testament to young people still remains an omnipresent concern today.

Finally, the election of Barack Obama to become the first African American President of the United States of America is the ultimate history-making accomplishment. President Obama's ascendancy illustrates the greatness of America and the pivotal role that education can play in the lives of individuals. He is a sterling example for all children that a quality education can make a significant difference in their lives. President Obama was born August 4, 1961, and completed his postsecondary education at Columbia University and Harvard Law School. Prior to becoming the 44th President of the United States, he served as a United States Senator from Chicago, Illinois. He assumed the Office of the Presidency on January 20, 2009, and later received the Nobel Peace Prize in October 2009. President Obama says that he recognizes the supreme importance of education and supports the need for accountability in schools.

While these are just a few of the individual successes, let us not forget that there were individuals behind each of the successes who helped to facilitate their ascendancy. It is the facilitator who helps encourage, who intervenes, who has the eagle eye of wisdom to know how to lead and guide students to success. The twenty-first century calls for more individuals who have knowledge and skills to lead, to cultivate the soil of human understanding, and to shepherd individuals safely to success.

What will be your contribution to the ages?

The twenty-first century, knowledge-based economy requires individuals who have knowledge in specific areas, who have appropriate skill sets, who are adaptable and flexible. These are in-demand skill sets that all students can develop by connecting them to their why. When asked why students are interested in a specific field, some say, "I want to find a cure to a disease that emaciated a loved one," or, "I want to make my parents proud," or even, "I want to give back to my parents." Every person can start his or her journey to transcendence and empowerment by embracing a greater passion and meaning in life with their why. Friedrich Nietzsche, a nineteenth-century German philosopher, said, "He who has a why to live can bear with almost any how." Among our many tasks is that of helping our students find the why and inspiring them to take ownership of their learning, to dream big dreams, and to accomplish extraordinary goals. Some will say, "It's too hard," but they have to learn to press beyond the comfort zone to accomplish their goals. Langston Hughes, one of the well-known poets of the Harlem Renaissance, was born in 1902. Yet, he must have understood the necessity of his voice for posterity. In his poem, "Mother to Son," Hughes speaks through the voice of a mother to communicate the message to African American youth that "Life has not been a crystal stair." Life has been difficult, but the youth are admonished that they must never give up. They must keep climbing.

Indicators of African American Student Success

———————— // ————————

This chapter provides indicators of success that practitioners can use to chart African American students' progressive Learning for Ownership growth. It also briefly presents 1) the framework for writing measurable objectives, and 2) pivot-point indicators of student success. The pivot points include students' attitudes, behaviors, ethos, achievement, self-perceptions, and perceptions held by others.

FRAMEWORK FOR WRITING AND
IDENTIFYING MEASURABLE RESULTS

When writing for measurable results, it is recommended that the expected outcomes be clearly identified. Some academicians start with the end goal in mind and work backwards to set realistic milestones and timelines. That is one approach. Others start at the beginning of the process and work through to the end. Regardless of the approach, benchmarks are essential for tracking goal attainment. They identify standards against which a person can compare or measure performance. Therefore, benchmarks are included in the Learning for Ownership Portfolio to help chart students' progress in pursuit of their goals. Periodically, it might be necessary to modify benchmarks based upon unforeseen circumstances that may occur.

In my review of data pertaining to public schools, the high dropout rates and low college and workforce-readiness rates among African American children surfaced as systemic problems nationally. Therefore, rectifying the problems would be a great indication of success. Rectifying the dropout problem, however, has a number of subcomponents that also require repair. For example, students drop out because of various reasons: their poor attendance, to pursue a job, low or failing grades, age, to get married, pregnancy, because they are suspended and/or expelled, because they do not meet the graduation requirements, or they drop out to enroll in a GED program. Each of the components might have different causes and need different solutions to fix the dropout problem. Learning for Ownership can help address and eventually correct the problems that directly pertain to education through the empowerment process. Other issues that pertain to family crises, employment issues, and other disruptive factors that lead to students dropping out must be addressed in concert with the appropriate social service agencies.

Additionally, the lack of college and workforce-readiness rates interferes with student success. In research reports in 2003 and also in 2010, the reports show that African American students fall behind all other ethnic categories of students in college and career readiness. While the results are not overwhelmingly positive for either of the groups in the study, the data still show African American students falling significantly behind all others. In the August 2010 ACT News entitled, "High School Core Course Selection Key to Success," the report indicates that "24 percent of all ACT-tested 2010 high school graduates met or surpassed all of ACT's college-readiness benchmarks." Only 4% of African American graduates met or surpassed the benchmarks. What does this mean? It means that 96 percent of the African American graduates tested did not score as college or career ready among the entire population. It also means that unless serious attention is given to rectifying the problems that interfere with student success, fewer students in general and fewer African American students in particular will be academically prepared to enroll in and complete college. According to results of national tests, African American students, upon graduation, are performing at the level of a white eighth-grade student in reading and a white seventh-grade student in math.

One can only wonder what happens during the school day and why so few children are gaining the knowledge, skills, and competencies required for success. These findings cause serious concerns about what is happening at school and raise questions about why students, across the board, are performing so poorly.

Following are pivot-point indicators of student success that teachers can use to track the impact of the Learning for Ownership Empowerment Model on each child to modify attitudes and behaviors and to enhance overall performance outcomes.

STUDENT ATTITUDES

Student attitudes make a significant difference in the caliber of their learning experience. Teachers are able to assess student attitudes rather easily. Consider, for example, how students respond when given classroom and/or homework assignments. Do students who previously had a negative attitude about school have more positive attitudes? This is certainly an indicator of success if students' attitudes have shifted from negative to positive. This positive shift should be acknowledged and students should be commended for their improvement. The accolades should be accompanied by reminders of the benefits that they will have as they consistently incorporate positive attitudes into their lives.

Based upon interviews with students, it is apparent that the attitudinal responses are often reflective of events that are happening in their lives at the moment. Therefore, survey results or other measures should chart students' attitudes over a period of time to ensure consistency. The consistent attitude demonstrated over time is a more reliable indicator of real and/or authentic change.

The Learning for Ownership Student Survey is one tool that can be administered as a pretest at the beginning of the semester and again as a post test during the middle of the semester to confirm whether students' attitudes have changed in a positive direction.

Some of the attitudes that teachers are expecting to observe in their students' Learning for Ownership journey are listed below. If the disposition is positive, the intent is to continue the positive attitudes. If attitudes begin to shift from positive to negative, the issues causing the shift should be discussed with students and interventions should be made quickly. Some of the items that focus on attitudes follow.

Checklist of Attitudes
Agree (+) Disagree (-)

- The student is cordial and pleasant.
- The student is compassionate and caring.
- The student has a positive attitude.
- The student engages in collaboration exercises easily.
- The student appears flexible and adaptable.
- The student works effectively as a member of a team.
- The student is courteous.

- The student is friendly.
- The student is receptive to constructive criticism.
- The student is eager to assist others.
- The student seems to like social interaction with peers.
- The student is respectful of others.

Teacher-led student conferences are recommended to help connect with each student on an individual basis, to troubleshoot issues and concerns, and to create a mentor-type relationship to further support students academically and psychologically.

Behaviors

The students' behaviors are also pivot-point indicators. The behaviors typically align with the attitudes. So, if the attitudes are more positive and the students see the benefits of school, they will more likely be motivated to learn, which will lead to change.

Some of the questions that practitioners can answer to assess a change in behaviors follow.

Checklist of Behaviors
Yes (+) No (-)

- Is the student's attendance record acceptable?
- Is the student submitting homework and class assignments?
- Is the student developing into a self-starter?
- Does the student seek help to understand and complete his work?
- Is the student actively engaged in his classes?

- Is the student participating in school activities?
- Does the student work well with others?
- Does the student volunteer to participate in class projects?
- Is the student flexible and adaptable?
- Is the student punctual for class?
- Does the student manage his time well?
- Is the student respectful of others?
- Is the student responsive to requests?
- Does the student demonstrate sufficient effort?
- Is the student responsible and reliable?
- Does the student demonstrate self-discipline?
- Is the student trustworthy?
- Is the student fair with others?

The attitudes and behaviors of students are usually influenced by those persons who are close to them (such as their peers and friends), those who love them (such as their family members), and by those whom they respect (such as their teachers, counselors, and other professionals). Therefore, positive, affirming feedback is vital. Additional factors that influence students' behaviors include the way students are treated in school, their interest in what they are learning, and their belief about the value of education.

ETHOS

The premise of Learning for Ownership is that students must develop the mindset and the skill sets to become responsible governors of their lives and of their future. During the developmental stages of their lives, they are in the progressive learning mode where they are acquiring the cognitive, affective, and psychomotor skills that, according to noted psychologist, Dr. Benjamin Bloom, aid in learning. Thus, as they mature and acquire more knowledge and experience, their decision making should be based more upon the cognitive, higher-order thinking skills rather than responding solely based upon their emotions or how they feel. The lack of development in the cognitive and affective domains has led many young individuals who otherwise had promising futures to a dead end: prison, death, or irreparable harm due to emotion-based decision making. The educational process helps groom students and prepares them to become more responsible in their decisions and in their choices.

As an indicator of African American student success, the ethos is significant to measure. The ethos is the driving force or the beliefs that students have that leads to success or failure. What do students believe about themselves, about others, and about the world around them? Do they believe all of the negative things that have been said about them? Do they believe all of the negative names they have been called? Or do they have an independent set of beliefs? And if they do have an independent set of beliefs, how did they acquire them?

Also, how many African American students can articulate their goals in life and their steps to goal attainment? Unfortunately, many students do not know what they want to become in life simply because they have not had the exposure to the realm of possibilities. Once they have identified their aspirations and decided they can attain their goals, they develop an unquenchable zeal. That newly acquired zeal that emanates from the ethos bolsters students' persistency in pursuit of their dreams. When students find their passion and their zeal, their motivation is unleashed. This is the high point that educators want to achieve with all students. Below are some of the ethos indicators.

Ethos Checklist
Yes (+) No (-)

- The student believes that others support him.

- The student believes that he can achieve his goals.

- The student believes his goals are attainable.

- The student believes he can make a positive contribution.

- The student believes his success will motivate others.

- The student believes his goal represents his purpose in life.

- The student believes that he has the ability.

- The student believes it is important to have a positive attitude.

- The student believes that his choices determine his future.

- The student believes he is the master of his fate.

ACHIEVEMENT

When students connect their learning to their passion, the educational process becomes more meaningful for them and a more enjoyable one for teachers. The students who have caught the vision become self-starters. They become devoted to their goals in life and begin making judgments about the people and the things in their lives that might interfere with their ability to achieve their goals. Following are some of the achievement-based indicators that can be used to identify whether students have embraced the vision of success.

<u>Achievement Indicators</u>
     Teacher's Comments

- What is the student's attendance record?
- Has the student attained grade-appropriate knowledge and skills in all subject areas?
- What are the student's grades?
- How have the student's grades changed?
- Does the student submit homework and class assignments by the due dates?
- What is the student's performance on standardized tests?

Teachers, counselors, principals, and other professionals know the students who are problem children. They know the troublemakers. Having been a high school teacher at one time in my career, I remember the under-the-breath remarks that were made when certain children approached. There were remarks, such as, "Here comes the kid who disrupted the class," and other similar comments. Without the student knowing, his reputation had spread throughout the school; and while the student might not have been in the classes of the other teachers, all of them, nonetheless, knew him. By the same token, when students do well, a similar informal network transmits messages about the success. "This child has really turned his life around," is a commonly used remark.

The perception held by others, particularly of teachers and counselors, is very important. When a student has been a poor performer or has been troubled emotionally and then makes a turnaround, it does not go unnoticed.

Self Perceptions

It is vital that students have self-efficacy to know that they can achieve their goals. It is the responsibility of parents to help them cultivate a belief in themselves and in their ability to achieve. Students' views of themselves are usually transparent and conveyed to others through their nonverbal gestures and actions. The poem, "You Can If You Think You Can," is attributed to several authors: Napoleon Hill, Walter D. Wintle, and C. W. Longenecker. The poem conveys the essence of a belief in self.

You Can If You Think You Can

If you think you are beaten, you are,
If you think you dare not, you don't
If you like to win, but you think you can't,
It is almost certain you won't.

If you think you'll lose, you're lost,
For out in the world we find,
Success begins with a fellow's will.
It's all in the state of mind.
If you think you are outclassed, you are,
You've got to think high to rise,
You've got to be sure of yourself before
You can ever win a prize.

Life's battles don't always go
To the stronger or faster man.
But soon or late the man who wins,
Is the man who thinks he can.

C. W. Longenecker

So, without question, a belief in self is vital to the steadfast pursuit of dreams and the ultimate attainment of them. Maintaining the proper attitude and behaviors during the process is key.

One way for students to gauge their daily attitude is through the use of the efficacy questions. Students have the option to respond to either of the two stems below. The decision point is for students, in consultation with their teachers, to decide how to address whatever issues might interfere with the teaching and learning process.

I AM READY to participate in class today because:
Decision Point:

or

I AM NOT READY to participate in class today because:
Decision Point:

PERCEPTIONS HELD BY OTHERS

The perception of others provides valuable information about the kinds of attitudes that are being detected that the student may or may not be aware of and may or may not want to convey. It is important for students to learn how to accept constructive criticism and feedback from others gracefully without feeling defensive, yet it is essential that they also differentiate among the people whose opinions and feedback of them they will accept and incorporate into a behavioral change. Some of the questions that are spinoffs of the pivot-point indicators follow:

Perceptions Held by Others:

- What are other professionals saying about the student's performance?

- What do others say about the behaviors of the student?

- What are the impressions that others have of the student?

- What are the nonverbal messages that the student is communicating to others?

OVERALL GROUP OUTCOME MEASURES

The overall performance of students should be compiled and presented as an indicator of change. The indicators will point to the success of the Learning for Ownership process that aids students in their academic and personal development. Some of the questions that point to indicators of success for the entire school are listed below.

Outcome Measures:

- What percentage of students are improving in their school performance?

- What is the grade distribution among students?

- What is the retention rate of students by grade level?

- What is the completion rate of students by grade level?

- What is the transition to college rate?

- What is the dropout rate trend?

- What is the teenage pregnancy trend?

- What percentage of high school students are enrolling in dual credit or are taking advanced placement courses?

- What percentage of students are passing the advanced placement tests?

- What percentage of students are reading at grade-appropriate levels?

- What percentage of students are graduating?
- What percentage of students are graduating with college-ready skills and workforce-ready skills?
- What percentage of students are transitioning to college?
- What percentage of students are performing well on standardized tests and other measures?

When extraordinary accomplishments are made by students, extraordinary efforts should be made to acknowledge their success and celebrate it. This can be done in various ways; but the acknowledgment helps inspire and motivate the students who have excelled. It also helps motivate and inspire others to also learn for ownership.

The indicators presented in this chapter are essential. The list is not all inclusive, as there might be indicators that some school districts have that vary slightly from this list. Nevertheless, the indicators listed are absolutely vital to measure the success of African American students as they embark upon learning for ownership. The checklists can be included in students' portfolios as a reminder of the expectations that teachers have of them.

Some might ask, "Why are the indicators necessary?" The indicators of success are necessary to adequately measure students' growth and attainment of knowledge, skills, and abilities. They are also a useful tool to help rectify the negative trends that are relegating many African American students to a substandard education, limited skills, and limited opportunities to contribute significantly to society.

Schools and Society Matter

This book has focused on learning for ownership and ways students can improve their mindsets and skill sets to enhance their education and their lives. The text has highlighted areas that are the core essentials to education and provided a typology for classification of student attitudes and a companion empowerment model for student improvement. This is the culminating chapter in the book and focuses on a societal imperative for change. What are the decisions that must be made about schools that will enhance learning for ownership for all students and that will ultimately impact society in positive ways? Individuals and organizations have discussed the ramifications of a business as usual approach to the future. Despite the numbers of students enrolled in schools, nationally, there are insufficient numbers with the appropriate skills and knowledge that society needs. Without marketable skills, what are the prospects for the majority of students, and what more can society do to help them? The challenge, if left unmet with appropriate interventions, will be devastating. Change is necessary in how we prepare students; otherwise, who will become the trained professionals, technicians, and great leaders of tomorrow? How committed are stakeholders to real, substantive change that will make a difference? Are the conversations for change authentic, or are the conversations merely opportunities for intellectual posturing? The actions taken will signal the authenticity and the commitment.

To begin the conversation for radical change, this chapter presents a proposal to pilot test a restructuring of urban school districts that have failing schools. The proposal is sure to incur resistance from those who will feel that their empires are being threatened, and it will gain support from those who will believe that their territories are being enlarged. This proposal which some might call "a modest proposal" takes into consideration the best interests of students, of schools, and of society.

THE STARTING POINT

First, let us lay the foundation before presenting the proposal. Momentarily reflect on the literature that is replete with statistics highlighting the issues and challenges that society faces due to academically under-prepared high school graduates. Many high school graduates are simply lacking the knowledge and the skills required for work or for college. Consider also the high dropout rates of students by the ninth grade. This number in and of itself is staggering and leaves society with individuals who, despite the investment made in them, will not have sufficient knowledge or skills to occupy a twenty-first century job. According to a report by the Alliance for Excellent Education Fact Sheet, February 2009, over a million students who enter ninth grade each fall fail to graduate in four years. This report is inclusive of all students, not just African Americans. The report also states that seven thousand students drop out every day. "Not only do the individuals themselves suffer," according to the report, "but each class of drop outs is responsible for substantial financial and social costs to the communities, states, and country in which they live." The data show that nationally, 71 percent of all students graduate from high school on time with a regular diploma; barely half of African American and Hispanic students graduate with their peers. On the revenue generation side, the report indicates that if US high schools and colleges raise the graduation rates of minorities—Hispanic, African American, and Native American students—to the levels of white students by 2020, the potential increase in personal income would add more than $310 billion to the US economy. But how can this happen when, according to Dr. Jay Greene of the Manhattan Public Policy Institute, only 9 percent of African American students actually graduate college ready. This low statistic is the same for Hispanic students. So, as reflected in the 2006 report of Alliance for Excellent Education, if the graduates do attend college, they will likely have to enroll in remedial education classes. Currently, 42 percent of community college freshman across the nation and 20 percent of freshmen at four-year institutions enroll in at least one remedial course according to the Alliance for Excellent Education Report.

As you can see, the problem is that too few students graduate from high schools with college-ready or workforce-ready skills. Unfortunately, the students do not, on the whole, test high enough for admission to most universities. When they apply for admission at community colleges, a high percentage of them have to take developmental and/or remedial courses in English, Mathematics, and reading before they are eligible to enroll in academic courses. This translates to mean that recent high school graduates have to repeat the college preparatory coursework they should have mastered in high school. The costs are high for school districts and taxpayers. Many students are shocked when they learn they have to take remedial courses in college. Their response is usually, "I took this course in high school. Retaking this course is a waste of my time," they say. This mounting cost is being paid twice by taxpayers. This practice in and of itself shows deficiencies and points to a level of ineffectiveness in the current system.

On the other hand, the data show good news about postsecondary institutions. Data reports show that students who complete a community college degree and transfer to a four-year institution as a junior perform just as well or better than those students who began at the university level as freshmen. This is, in large part, due to the aligned curricula, highly credentialed faculty in their teaching fields, and student engagement in their learning.

The restructuring of public schools that is presented here will help prepare students for success. It will add value to society through the trained talent pool that will be available for work. It will result in new taxpayers and productive citizens who will become consumers of the goods and services that society produces.

The Learning for Ownership Empowerment Model that was presented earlier will help change the mindsets and skill sets of students to improve their attitudes and their performance levels. The radical change proposal will provide the immediate motivation and incentive for students to persist in school and to excel.

What Does Society Need?

Society needs better-educated, well-trained individuals to fill jobs and to keep the engines of the society working and moving smoothly. There is a need for more well-educated and well-trained individuals to fill new jobs, replacement jobs, and vacant jobs. The society needs individuals with intellect and the ability to make decisions and lead our institutions at all levels in the public and private sectors. Implementation of the proposal will lead to a major change in the performance of students and to outcomes-based results within two to five years. This chapter presents a momentum shift that could turn the tide for the education of African American children and their ability to become major contributors to the future of society.

An Example of Revolutionary Change

Consider the number of students who completed high school with workforce certifications and associate's degrees prior to 1990. There were very few, if any. Now, consider the number of students who, after 1990, have completed certifications or associate's degrees by the time of high school graduation. The numbers are in the hundreds of thousands. The Tech Prep and Dual Credit Movements are the reasons for the increase, resulting in more college attendance and college completion among students of all ethnicities.

At the beginning of the Dual Credit Movement, there was resistance from the educational purists who thought young people could not compete with older, more adult students on the college level. Many purists were also focused on the seat time requirements and the history of tradition and *the way it has always been done* argument to make their case. Some high school teachers were also resistant to change due to fears of losing their jobs. All of the fears were unfounded. The fears that will be associated with the proposed pilot will also be unfounded. In fact, the proposal to restructure public schools will instead create a renaissance in public education. The school reform will renew the interests among students in school; it will meet the needs of society, and it will help curtail the rapid increase in social problems that plague society.

Most readers would agree that when there is ample evidence that systems are broken, there is a need to evaluate the system and then decide to either repair, renovate, or replace the system. That is what this chapter introduces to the reader: an option that can be implemented to improve the system of education for students and to achieve enhanced benefits for society.

The Radical Change Proposal

There are two parts to the radical change proposal. In part one, I propose that the role and purpose of public school education be redefined and streamlined to prepare students in grades one through ten years of school for a high school diploma. This means students would complete a high school diploma in ten years instead of twelve.

Immediately, some might say, "How can students complete the curriculum in ten years when they are not learning the skills required in twelve?" That is precisely the point. Students are not learning the skill sets in twelve years, as demonstrated earlier. That is the reason many entering freshmen at community and technical colleges as well as open-admissions universities are enrolled in remedial courses. There is a need for public schools to re-evaluate their curriculum and streamline it as necessary. They should work with postsecondary institutions to align their student-transfer curriculum and introduce more substantive preparation in science, technology, engineering, and mathematics (STEM). The curriculum should retain a focus on reading, writing, oral and written communication and create a greater emphasis on teaching critical thinking skills. Finally, there is a need to retrain teachers to become more transformative educators who are credentialed in their teaching fields. The benefits can be calculated in dollars and cents. Think about the comments made by people who desire change. Are your sentiments similar?

- Twelve years of schooling is an antiquated concept that has proven to be ineffective.

- Twelve years of schooling is perhaps a political issue that continues the flow of dollars to districts based upon the way it has always been.

- Businesses are not getting better employees.

- Colleges and universities are not getting better students.
- Tax dollars are dwindling, and the pipeline of new taxpayers is not being replenished.

If you agree with the statements, what are your plans to initiate change? With the proposed structure, public schools can begin to refocus on their role, purpose, vision, and mission as the first-level educational provider. They can decide the instructional curricula and pedagogy, methodology, and assessment of learning outcomes for twenty-first-century learners who will seamlessly transition to a postsecondary institution. Being in public school for twelve years until the student is seventeen or eighteen is a twentieth-century model that no longer has merit in the twenty-first century. Students are more mature, and society is more fast paced and more in need of individuals with knowledge and talent than ever before. A re-examination of the public school curriculum should be conducted to identify what is needed to prepare students for multiple educational options and career pathways in demand by society and that will result in a robust educational system where students learn the twenty-first-century knowledge and skills to be globally competitive.

In part two of the radical change proposal, I recommend that all students who graduate after ten years of schooling automatically become the new college and university students. It is reasonable that these students be supported by redirected tax dollars for two years to enroll in postsecondary institutions to pursue and complete a certificate or a two-year degree. Upon completion, the graduates have the option to go to work in a high-demand field or to continue their education toward a higher degree at their expense.

Some naysayers might chime in and say that African American and /or minority students would largely fall into the trap of a technical degree. What a wonderful trap to fall into, particularly if it allows for gainful employment and a livable wage. Think about the seven thousand students who are dropping out of school every day. Those seven thousand dropouts could likely become a severe drain on taxpayers. The data show that "Over the course of a lifetime, a high school dropout will earn, on average, about $260,000 less than a high school graduate." Minority students today are graduating from high school without any credentials and without sufficient skills to go to work or to college.

BENEFITS

The benefits of the proposed plan are excellent for students, for society, and for the public schools. Instructors who are currently working in the public schools but who do not have the credentials to teach academic courses will need to return to the university to upgrade their credentials as required by the accrediting and licensing agencies.

This plan will allow for a renewed vibrancy in society and a lessening of the fears about the future. The outcomes will reflect the following:

- Students will be preparing for a career earlier in their educational experience.
- Fewer employable individuals will be out of work.
- Fewer businesses will have the challenge of finding a well-trained talent pool for work.
- Fewer individuals will have to resort to radical means to get money to support their families.
- The crime rate might be reduced as a result of more individuals having skills for work.

The process described allows students to energetically and enthusiastically learn for ownership. The public school and post-secondary curricula would be more robust and learner centered. Students would know that by the time they are sixteen years of age, they will be in college and by the time they are eighteen years of age, they will be degree holders and fully prepared for gainful employment or ready to transition to a baccalaureate degree program.

The New Image of Schools

The radical change proposal will improve the image of public schools and will result in a strategic new direction for society. Problems that have troubled schools and school districts will diminish. The proposed change can be the pivotal turning point for society.

Rationale

As tax dollars dwindle, the public must decide how much of their resources will be continuously funneled into an educational system that is not producing the desired results. With the radical-change proposal, a new generation of taxpayers will be regenerating society on a regular basis due to their early training, their earlier employment in in-demand jobs, and their income generated that will allow them to pay taxes and help fuel the economy. We will see within a two-to-five-year period higher employment, more regeneration of businesses, and a jump start to the economy. School districts, though restructured, would retain their independence. Teachers who are currently teaching eleventh and twelfth grades could upgrade their credentials and be retooled to teach at postsecondary levels.

The Downside

There are no negatives associated with this concept. It will become a political issue that will need to be addressed, and legislation will need to be developed to advance the proposed agenda. Obviously, the curricular demands can be met by postsecondary institutions.

Some might ask, "What will happen with the first ten years of schooling? Will school districts be able to meet the proposed challenge?" Yes, they can! A major impediment would be the naysayers who fear change. Fear of change often stands in the way of progress.

Learning for Ownership

What will this change mean for African American children to learn for ownership? It will capture the interest of students to work harder to achieve real goals that are not so distant into their future. They will also see the relevancy of what they are learning to their career goals. More students will have a certification or degree; and best of all, they will also have viable options. In the end analysis, students will be able to take greater possession of their lives and prepare for career fields that will create great livelihoods for them.

Why Do Institutions Exist?

In my estimation, institutions are a product of society, and they exist to serve the needs of society. Public schools and postsecondary schools are examples of institutions. When those institutions are broken and no longer function properly, they are not benefitting the society that they were established to support.

Society is now at a crossroads. The minority populations will soon become the majority populations in many urban cities in the United States, yet many of those same populations are not being educated sufficiently to become a positive contributor to society. It is now time for all institutions to reevaluate their effectiveness and determine their value to society.

A CALL TO SOCIETY FOR ACTION

The prospects for the future are exciting, and the expected outcomes are anticipated to be phenomenal. Now is the time, and this is the generation to usher in a change that will benefit all of society. Schools and society matter, and the decisions that both entities make at this juncture in history will determine the future of America. This shift will accelerate the Learning for Ownership process for all students. Students will have the opportunity to become empowered literally and figuratively. Learning for Ownership's success is not dependent upon the radical restructuring of schools for its validation. The validation occurs with each student when the mindset is renewed and the skill set is developed. The restructuring of schools will become a natural motivator, however, that will encourage more students to stay in school to achieve. The Learning for Ownership process will help, in this instance, to serve as the catalyst to sustain students' drive academically, socially, and emotionally. Regardless of the school's structure, it is time for African American students to become tenacious in pursuit of a quality education that will surely add enormous value to their lives. It is also the hour for educational practitioners to use their talents and abilities unreservedly to prepare world-class students. So, how will the next century report the progress of our efforts to transform generations of individuals? The report will depend upon the commitment and the actions that we take, both individually and collectively, to develop the human capital of our nation to its fullest potential. In the end analysis, I concur with the statement made by Frederick Douglass, editor of the most influential black newspaper of the mid 19th century. He said, "It is easier to build strong children than to repair broken men." Now decide. What role will you play?

Bibliography

Abbott, John and Terry Ryan. "Learning to go with the Grain of the Brain." <u>Education Canada</u>. Spring 1999.

Alliance for Excellent Education. "African-American Students and U. S. high Schools." Fact Sheet. April 2007.

American College Testing Service. 2005 Report.

Aristotle's Ethics. Stanford Encyclopedia of Philosophy. (online) http://plato.stanford.edu/entries/aristotle-ethics/.

Dewey, John. "My Pedagogic Creed." School Journal. Vol. 54 (Jan. 1897).

Ellison, Ralph. *Invisible Man.* New York. The New American Library. 1952.

Fincher-Ford, Margaret L. *High School Students Earning College Credit: A Guide to Creating Dual Credit Programs. Thousand Oaks.* Corwin Press. 1996.

Frankyl, Victor E. *Man's Search for Meaning*. New York. Pocket Book. 1973.

Freire, Paulo. *Pedagogy of the Oppressed*. New York. The Continuum Publishing Company. 1994.

Funderstanding (online). Brain-Based Research. Funderstanding.com. 1998-2008.

Goleman, Daniel. *Social Intelligence: The New Science of Human Relationships*. New York. Bantam Books, 2006.

Greene, J. P. and Winters, M. "Public High School Graduation and College Readiness: 1991-2002." New York: Manhattan Institute for Public Policy Research.

Henley, William Ernest. "Invictus." 1888.

Hilliard, Asa. Egyptologist. 2005.

http://www.thebowencenter.org/pages/conceptfpp.html.

Ingersoll, Richard M. "Core Problems: Out-of-Field Teaching Persists in Key Academic Courses in High-Poverty Schools." The Education Trust. November 2008.

NCREL and Metiri Group. "enGauge 21st Century Skills: Literacy in the Digital Age." (online).

Sapir, Edward. "Conceptual Categories in Primitive Languages." Science. 1931.

SCANS (Secretary's Commission on Achieving Necessary Skills). U. S. Department of Labor, 1990.

Shade, B. J. "Culture: The Key to Adaptation." In B. J. Shade (ed.), *Culture, Style and the Educative Process*. Springfield. 1989.

Thorndike, E. L. "Intelligence and its Uses." Harper's Magazine. 1920.

U. S. Census Bureau. (2008 and 2009). U. S. data by age, sex, race, ethnic origin.

Washington, Booker T. *Up From Slavery*. New York. Barnes and Noble, 2003.